STRUGGLES
OF A MAN

A daily
walk
with God

John M. Maisel

Regal
Books

A Division of GL Publications
Ventura, CA U.S.A.

The foreign language publishing of all Regal books is under the direction of Gospel Litera-ture International (GLINT). GLINT provides financial and technical help for the adapta-tion, translation and publishing of books for millions of people worldwide. For information regarding translation, contact: GLINT, P.O. Box 6688, Ventura, California 93006.

Scripture quotations in this publication, unless otherwise indicated are from the *New Inter-national Version,* Holy Bible. Copyright © 1978 by New York International Bible Society. Used by permission. Other versions quoted include:
Phillips—The New Testament in Modern English, Revised Edition, J.B. Phillips, Translator. © J.B. Phillips 1958, 1960, 1972. Used by permission of Macmillan Publishing Co., Inc.
RSV—Revised Standard Version, copyrighted 1946 and 1952 by the Division of Christian Education of the NCCC, U.S.A., and used by permission.
KJV—The Authorized King James Version.

Library of Congress Cataloging in Publication Data
    Maisel, John, 1940-
      Struggles of a man.

      Includes index.
        1. Christian life—1960-   2. Maisel,
John, 1940-   I. Title.
BV4501.2.M329   248.4   82-80006
ISBN 0-8307-0837-5   AACR2

FOREWORD

One of the greatest weaknesses in most men is being open and honest. Transparency is considered weakness! Culture supports this point of view and the male ego seems to maintain it.

In this respect, John Maisel's *The Struggles of a Man* is refreshing and encouraging. Here is a man who is willing—publicly—to be open and honest, yet with discretion. Every living adult male—and female—will identify with John's own struggles and efforts at living the Christian life Bible style!

Several years ago I wrote *The Measure of a Man* and in many respects I see this book, *The Struggles of a Man,* as a sequel. Not one of us will ever measure up to God's standards without a struggle. The Apostle Paul affirmed this in many instances in his own writings. And any biblical character I've ever studied and every Christian I've ever known has gone through a process—often painful— to arrive at maturity in Christ. And, of course, that process never ends while one is on this earth.

I also had the privilege of reading John's first efforts at putting these thoughts and talks to God on paper. I've watched the process of seeing his final manuscript emerge. I'm excited to recommend it. It will help you and encourage you in your own journey towards maturity and "measuring up!"

PREFACE

The contents of this book are the results of a diary I have kept as an active businessman, over a 10-year period. I never had any intention of making public any of these conversations between myself and God, due to the personal nature of many of them. But because of the encouragement of several men who had access to them I have placed them in book form.

These notes to God are simply the outworking of everyday situations which involve the internal struggles that each Christian faces in the marketplace of life. They reveal my defeats and failures, as well as my victories and successes. I hope as I share these personal times with you that you will conclude, as I have, that Christ is sufficient in whatever circumstances of life you may find yourself.

DEDICATION

To my wife Susie who knows and understands me better than I do myself sometimes and still loves and accepts me—and to my favorite daughter A'dina who brings great joy to my life in just being her unique spontaneous self.

Abundance

Living Like a Bum or Millionaire

If I believe the fact that I have one million dollars in my checking account, I will act like a millionaire. If the fact of the million dollars is true, but I don't believe it and act in accordance with my disbelief, I will live like a bum.

With Christ, as with the bank, all the life and wealth you have, Father, is available to me. I must now act according to the promise which says I have been given everything that is needed for life and for godly living.

His divine power has given us everything we need for life and godliness through our knowledge of him who called us by his own glory and goodness (2 Peter 1:3).
And you have been given fullness in Christ, who is the head over every power and authority (Colossians 2:10).

ANGER

The Stronghold of Bitterness

I'm angry because of an argument with my wife. I must work through the situation to gain the proper attitude.

My resentment and bitterness, Father, have grieved your Spirit within me—and my wife. I have said my way is better than your way of kindness, gentleness and meekness. In my pride and arrogance I have concluded that my understanding will accomplish my objectives better than your way.

Your Word says that contention comes only by pride. That makes it simple and points directly to me in regard to my argument with my dear wife.

Only by pride cometh contention: but with the well advised is wisdom (Proverbs 13:10, KJV).
He guides the humble in what is right and teaches them his way (Psalm 25:9).

When Anger Is Free to Run

I have been truly angry lately with those around me. It seems, Father, when I feel wronged that my reaction is determined by whom I'm focusing my attention on: you or the other person.

Thank you for bringing these difficult matters into my life, because these people are simply revealing my sinful spirit; they are not the cause of it.

For man's anger does not bring about the righteous life that God desires (James 1:20).

ATTITUDE

A Sense of Uselessness

I'm feeling . . .
. . . a lack of purpose,
. . . that the job could run without me,
. . . that I cause tension at home.

So, back to the question of Why? Why my unbelief? Why my sense of uselessness? I have no desire to reach out and even believe the truth. I don't even want to write these words to you. I must understand that I do *"receive it all by faith,"* even when, as now, I *feel* as if I have received nothing. My attitude of believing must be that of actively receiving and behaving upon what you will for my life.

If I say I believe that Christ lives in me, I need to *act with expectation* that this is happening. Feelings contrary to this are a lie, and I must treat them as a lie. The correct attitude causes me not to focus on a self-pitying Why, but on the joy of Christ now.

Why then did you bring me out of the womb? (Job 10:18).
I cry out to God Most High, to God, who fulfills his purpose for me (Psalm 57:2).

BOLDNESS

With the Right Attitude

I'm on the way to the airport and I sense a deep freedom that will enable me to share the gospel with boldness. I sense these attitudes in my spirit which will give me this freedom:

1. I need not worry about what the person will think of me, whether I will be liked or disliked, whether I will appear cool or uncool.

2. I seem not to be uptight about whether the person will or will not respond to your message.

These attitudes allow me to be totally free to relax and simply be ready to tell the gospel. I trust you will develop all that needs to happen.

Therefore, since we have such a hope, we are very bold (2 Corinthians 3:12).
It is written: "I believed; therefore I have spoken." With that same spirit of faith we also believe and therefore speak (2 Corinthians 4:13).

CHRISTLIKENESS

Year-End Inventory

It is the last day of another year. What a shame to end the year in anger and bitterness, but I sense both in my spirit. I have gone through some terrible financial difficulties. They have taken the puff out of my pride and have caused my spirit to be truly submissive. I can't seem to do anything right, Father, and there is a rebellious attitude in me. I am a son who finds fault with his heavenly Father's wisdom.

You, Father, whose love is perfect, whose way is tried, whose faithfulness is everlasting to everlasting—you, who made and are molding me, are only doing in me that which I ask for. I ask that your best be accomplished in my life, then I become rebellious when you put me through some necessary surgery. Actually, that is the very thing I have requested—to be conformed to Christ's likeness.

My sin of pride and unbelief has been placed upon you, Lord Jesus. Thank you.

And we know that in all things God works for the good of those who love him, who have been called according to his purpose. For those God foreknew he also predestined to be conformed to the likeness of his Son, that he might be the firstborn among many brothers (Romans 8:28,29).
For we are God's workmanship, created in Christ Jesus to do good works, which God prepared in advance for us to do (Ephesians 2:10).

Reality Is Christ

Today I want to visualize Christ; for what He is, I am to become. What He does, I ought to do. As I see Him walk and act, so am I to walk and act. Colossians 2:13 says that you have made me "alive with Christ." And, "He forgave [me] all [my] sins."

Reality is Christ.

So then, just as you received Christ Jesus as Lord, continue to live in him (Colossians 2:6).
Whoever claims to live in him must walk as Jesus did (1 John 2:6).

When My Walk Does Not Match My Talk

Lord, you say to me, "Follow Me. Follow my way."

I see few qualities in my life that would give me the assurance that I am following you.

I do see the results of following my way, however; and these manifest a lack of love, no inspiration, and selfish ambition.

"Come, follow me," Jesus said, "and I will make you fishers of men" (Mark 1:17).
Then he said to them all: "If anyone would come after me, he must deny himself and take up his cross daily and follow me" (Luke 9:23).

COMMITMENT

God's Use of a Man

It is true that you can only use a man who has the right kind of heart attitude. Why then do I spend more time focusing on my ministry and my reputation in that ministry than I do dealing with myself openly and honestly? I should be trusting you to use me in your timing and in any way you choose.

I fear that much of my attitude comes from thoughts of what I am doing for you and how this will be viewed by other Christians, rather than just doing what you want me to do.

For the eyes of the Lord range throughout the earth to strengthen those whose hearts are fully committed to him (2 Chronicles 16:9).

The Tension of Selfishness

MY selfish desire is to keep my company here in Dallas for:

MY convenience,

MY position,

MY success,

MY recognition.

However, a decision must be made about the ultimate future of the company based on what is best for the company and what is best for the other partners who desire to see it moved.

Thank you, Father, that in the midst of all this emotional struggle your ultimate desire will be done.

Commit to the Lord whatever you do, and your plans will succeed. The Lord works out everything for his own ends (Proverbs 16:3,4).

A Simple Prayer

Lord, this is my prayer to you, "Not my will, but your will be done."

Guide me as a son who simply says, "Father, I trust you with my life."

I want to do what you want me to do. I yield myself up to you so you can have the freedom you need to lead me in your path of righteousness, which you have creatively prepared for each one of your sons and daughters.

I cry out to God Most High, to God, who fulfills his purpose for me (Psalm 57:2).
When I said, "My foot is slipping," your love, O Lord, supported me. When anxiety was great within me, your consolation brought joy to my soul (Psalm 94:18,19).

Hard Questions that God Asks

I see you asking me today, Jesus, if I am willing to empty myself of everything and allow you to be my only possession.

Help me to find pleasure and joy in you no matter what my activity.

You, Lord Jesus, who is Wisdom, tell me that wisdom "is more precious than rubies; nothing you desire can compare with her."

King David said he desired nothing more than to behold you!

Teach me to see you clearly today in every situation and circumstance you bring to me.

Those who look to him are radiant; their faces are never covered with shame (Psalm 34:5).
You have made known to me the path of life; you will fill me with joy in your presence, with eternal pleasures at your right hand (Psalm 16:11).

The Proper Place for Expectation

Lord, whenever something enters my life, whether actions, words or reactions, help my first response to be to focus inwardly on you, for you are my life.

This self-control will allow me the freedom of not being in bondage to the situation, because my inward eye is only on the person of Christ. My only expectation will be from you and not from another person or situation.

David said about him: "I saw the Lord always before me. Because he is at my right hand, I will not be shaken" (Acts 2:25).
Let us throw off everything that hinders and the sin that so easily entangles, and let us run with perseverance the race marked out for us. Let us fix our eyes on Jesus, the author and perfecter of our faith (Hebrews 12:1,2).

The Heart Which Determines Lasting Value

It appears that what a Ph.D., athlete, congressman, actor or some other celebrity has to say about Christ and the Christian life is better received than what one says who is not a celebrity. The plain, simple, ordinary man whom you may have touched in a special way may have a special message from you. But because he is "ordinary," we don't listen. Lord, I mustn't fall into the trap of thinking this is your point of view just because many people believe this fallacy.

It is the heart that is completely surrendered to you which creates applause in heaven, not whether the person possesses an acceptable criterion of success or not.

One viewpoint gains the applause and glory of man; the other gains the secret praise and applause of you.

The key here is that I must advance your ministry, not according to the principles of the world, but according to your ways. If my ultimate desire is to please you, I will do it your way. If my goal is to promote myself, then I will do it the world's way with maybe limited success, or even worse, with great success!

. . . poor, yet making many rich; having nothing, and yet possessing everything (2 Corinthians 6:10)
Calling his disciples to him, Jesus said, "I tell you the truth, this poor widow has put more into the treasury than all the others. They all gave out of their wealth; but she, out of her poverty, put in everything—all she had to live on" (Mark 12:43,44).

Commitment That Will Last

Most men look for a cause.
Most causes last only a few years.
My commitment is to a cause that will last for eternity.

. . . according to his eternal purpose which he accomplished in Christ Jesus our Lord (Ephesians 3:11).
The Lord foils the plans of the nations; he thwarts the purposes of the peoples. But the plans of the Lord stand firm forever, the purposes of his heart through all generations (Psalm 33:10,11).

What If Everyone Turned Against Me?

I wonder what my commitment would be to you, Lord, if all the Christian community turned on me—if all the world despised me? Jesus, you knew the reality of this and you responded by faith in a desire to glorify the Father.

Should this ever happen to me, my only hope is in your Lordship in my life.

But how is it to your credit if you receive a beating for doing wrong and endure it? But if you suffer for doing good and you endure it, this is commendable before God (1 Peter 2:20).

At my first defense, no one came to my support, but everyone deserted me. May it not be held against them (2 Timothy 4:16).

He was despised and rejected by men, a man of sorrows, and familiar with suffering (Isaiah 53:3).

CONFESSION

My Greatest Need—Love

I am walking in unbelief.

I am anxious, fatigued and worried today.

I find that such sins as these cause anger and reactions to situations which trust and rest in you would never cause.

My eyes have been on everyone and everything but you. Father, may the grace of Jesus be with my spirit, that there may be freedom and so your Spirit can produce your love in me.

If there is ever a need in my life, it is learning how to love.

Be devoted to one another in brotherly love. Honor one another above yourselves (Romans 12:10).
I said, "O Lord, have mercy on me; heal me, for I have sinned against you" (Psalm 41:4).

CONSCIENCE

Fear Caused By Misunderstanding

Many of man's fears are founded on wrong attitudes. For example, Joe came by today and said he had a certain fear every time he saw me because he felt he had wronged me. It is interesting to see that his bondage with this idea was based upon what he thought I was thinking about him when, in reality, *the thought had never entered my mind.* When he said he felt as if he had wronged me, I had to ask him to explain what he meant.

But, Lord, I have done the same thing. If I believe a person is thinking a bad thing about me, and his opinion is important to me, I tend to change my behavior to impress him so he will think differently about me. Of course, the problem with this is that most of the time people aren't thinking the thoughts about me I think they are.

I must change this behavioral pattern. The only place to change it is in having a conscience void of offense to you and man.

But do this with gentleness and respect, keeping a clear conscience, so that those who speak maliciously against your good behavior in Christ may be ashamed of their slander" (1 Peter 3:16).
So I strive always to keep my conscience clear before God and man (Acts 24:16).

CONTRITION

Praying with a Broken Heart

This weekend was a traumatic experience. It was the first time I have ever prayed with a broken heart. I sensed some of the deep hurt that Christ must have felt when rejected by the people He chose to die for. Oh, what love to be rejected and still be willing to die for those who rejected Him!

Father, it has been a privilege to communicate with you from a broken and contrite heart. Grant me, I pray, a beautiful spirit, pure motives and genuine love for your name's sake in this situation. My defense is in you and is you. I can see you taking away assets from me for the purpose of restoring them in the future, if you choose, so that I might possibly be faithfully used for your glory.

The sacrifices of God are a broken spirit; a broken and contrite heart, O God, you will not despise (Psalm 51:17).
"Has not my hand made all these things, and so they came into being?" declares the Lord. "This is the one I esteem: he who is humble and contrite in spirit, and trembles at my word" (Isaiah 66:2).
Why are you downcast, O my soul? Why so disturbed within me? Put your hope in God, for I will yet praise him, my Savior and my God (Psalm 42:11).

COVETING

The Focus of the Eyes

Much is said about the lust of the flesh and the pride of life from 1 John 2, but little is said about the lust of the eyes. I think the core problem of lustful eyes is when we focus on coveting what others have. If we could overcome this covetousness, we would learn the truth of contentment as a quality of life. We do not automatically have your perspective to know that "godliness with contentment is great gain." We have to learn it.

Paul learned to be content in whatever state he was in. To be content in this way, Father, I need to know that to be in your will is the most blessed place to be no matter what the environment, even if it's the cross. I need to learn to focus on what I *have*—not on what I *don't have*. This will be the key to contentment!

You give me your shield of victory, and your right hand sustains me; you stoop down to make me great (Psalm 18:35).
Praise the Lord, O my soul, and forget not all his benefits (Psalm 103:2).

When I Tend to Covet

As I look around, I tend to covet other's ministries, services and, most of all, that you are using them more than me. What I am seeing is the thrill of their work and their public acclaim. You bring me back to the words of Paul in Romans 12:3, "Don't cherish exaggerated ideas of yourself or your importance, but try to have a sane estimate of your capabilities by the light of the faith that God has given to you all" (*Phillips*). If I have the privilege of being used, the key word for me then should be "contentment" in ministry.

Jesus, you say to *follow* you—PERIOD.

Then Peter turned round and noticed the disciple whom Jesus loved following behind them. . . . So he said, "Yes, Lord, but what about him?"
"If it is my wish," returned Jesus, "for him to stay until I come, is that your business, Peter? You must follow me" (John 21:20, 22, Phillips).

DECISIONS

The Fear of Confrontation

I don't want to talk to Bill today. The motive seems to be fearing a confrontation which would force me into making a business decision which could be the wrong one. This fear of not wanting to make a wrong decision must come from a perfectionist attitude. Some of the times that I do not want to make any mistakes may be rooted in my feelings of inferiority.

Father, I must learn not to focus on the situation, but on your presence and the fact that your will is being worked out.

"Because he loves me," says the Lord,. . . "he will call upon me, and I will answer him; I will be with him in trouble, I will deliver him and honor him" (Psalm 91:15).

How to Make Correct Decisions

The key to what I believe is the basis of how I make decisions. Decision-making must start from a point of reference: that there is one absolute God who controls the world according to His purpose and who works for my personal benefit. Lord, this thought is comforting when I make business decisions which don't accomplish my immediate goals, but which do accomplish your eternal results.

I know your commitment to me is not based upon what I do, but in what attitude and spirit I do it. What you have been doing in teaching me this shows me that it is an insult to you to think that you can't solve my problems. The reason I have been afraid to release myself to you is that I want to appear better than I am. But until I give you the ownership of my life, I can't be relaxed.

For a man's ways are in full view of the Lord, and he examines all his paths (Proverbs 5:21).
Turn my heart toward your statutes and not toward selfish gain (Psalm 119:36).

The Struggle in Decision-Making

When I feel I need to be loved physically, I have two frames of reference to consider before making a decision.

Your truth acknowledges that the need is real and that you desire me to meet these physical needs. You have also given the pattern in which I can have true fulfillment—and that is within the confines of my marriage.

Satan's frame of reference is that the wife cannot meet man's needs so they must only be met by another woman. Satan's way is always the easy way to have momentary fulfillment with a long-term consequence. It deals only with the now—with temporal pleasure.

Though your way is hard for me many times, it is the way which brings present fulfillment with lasting achievement for your purpose in my character development.

The key issue, when confronted with such a decision as seeking out the love of a woman, is which frame of reference do I choose to believe. Do I believe and act on your truth which brings the reward of righteousness or the lie of Satan which brings the consequence of compromise?

Father, in grace alone, keep my way pure before you.

Enjoy life with your wife, whom you love (Ecclesiastes 9:9).
Blessed is the man who does not walk in the counsel of the wicked or stand in the way of sinners or sit in the seat of mockers (Psalm 1:1).
Can a man scoop fire into his lap without his clothes being burned? Can a man walk on hot coals without his feet being scorched? So is he who sleeps with another man's wife; no one who touches her will go unpunished (Proverbs 6:27-29).

EDIFYING

My Words Do Hurt You

Lord Jesus, you asked Saul of Tarsus why he was persecuting you.

Saul wasn't hating or beating or resenting you physically, but only those who believed in you. But because believers are the Body of Christ, you received the attitudes and actions of Saul as though they had been done to you personally.

My attitudes and actions to those in the Body must also be seen as if they are being done to you personally. Help me, Father, to lift up my brothers and sisters in order to edify them to others instead of tearing them down.

I boast somewhat freely about the authority the Lord gave us for building you up rather than pulling you down (2 Corinthians 10:8).
This is why I write these things when I am absent, that when I come I may not have to be harsh in my use of authority—the authority the Lord gave me for building you up, not for tearing you down (2 Corinthians 13:10).

ENEMIES

Developing the Right Kind of Enemies

Why do we feel uncomfortable around certain people? Many times it is because they have a standard that is higher than ours, and that is threatening. This was one reason the religious leaders rejected and despised you, Jesus. They were uncomfortable with your quality of life. You threatened the standard that had become comfortable to them. But the people who knew themselves as sinners were attracted to you.

Lord, this teaches me that I need to have the right kind of enemies more than the right kind of friends.

Do you think I came to bring peace on earth? No, I tell you, but division (Luke 12:51).

Here is a glutton and a drunkard, a friend of tax collectors and "sinners" (Matthew 11:19).

Woe to you, teachers of the law and Pharisees, you hypocrites! You are like whitewashed tombs, which look beautiful on the outside but on the inside are full of dead men's bones and everything unclean (Matthew 23:27).

ETERNITY

Learning to Rule for Eternity

Jesus said, "The Father loves me because I lay down my life."

One of your purposes for your children is to prepare us to rule in eternity. In order to learn how to rule in the Kingdom, our primary lessons come in the area of the character development of my soul. Therefore, you are more concerned with my life and its response to the situation you put me in than my outward acclaim in the areas of ministry and business.

My conflicts in the home and business world and how I handle them might be more important to my learning how to rule in the Kingdom properly than my accomplishing great things for you in my public ministry. Though I may want those visible accomplishments, they may not be the *best* you have planned for me, for your way concerns the goal of preparing me to share your rule for eternity. This is why so many of the "last" shall be first, because there have been those who have quietly submitted to your way of preparation for them on earth—no matter what their circumstances—for their eventual position to rule in the Kingdom. The first shall be last because we thought ministry was equated with spirituality—how false!

"I tell you the truth," he said, "this poor widow has put in more than all the others. All these people gave their gifts out of their wealth; but she out of her poverty put in all she had to live on" (Luke 21:3,4).
Blessed and holy are those who have part in the first resurrection. The second death has no power over them, but they will be priests of God and of Christ and will reign with him for a thousand years (Revelation 20:6).

EXCELLENCE

The Good Versus the Best

Father, give me a discerning spirit between what is *good* in the business community and what is *best* in the halls of the Kingdom!

We have the tendency to feel that you are happy with us because we are involved in an activity that is thought well of by other Christians. I fear that many of the activities I'm involved in will be considered only as wood, hay and stubble from your point of view.

Lord, we need to see that meekness is greater than self-confidence—humility and gentleness are greater than arrogance and pride—a forbearing spirit is more commendable than a competitive spirit.

Let your gentleness be evident to all (Philippians 4:5).
If any man builds on this foundation using gold, silver, costly stones, wood, hay or straw, his work will be shown for what it is, because the Day will bring it to light. It will be revealed with fire, and the fire will test the quality of each man's work (1 Corinthians 3:12,13).
Whatever is true, whatever is noble, whatever is right, whatever is pure, whatever is lovely, whatever is admirable—if anything is excellent or praiseworthy—think about such things (Philippians 4:8).

FAILURE

Dealing With Failure in Your Top Priority

After having an insightful time in your Word—Galatians 2:20—this morning, I ruined things by getting angry with my wife.

This defeat in your top priority, my relationship with my wife, makes me almost ready to give up. Though I am a man indwelt by you according to your Word; though I am freed to be empowered by you according to your promise; and though I'm freed to be guided by you as I trust you—yet I am not allowing myself to be controlled by you because of my own pride.

Father, my mind knows your ways, but my will at times is weak and undisciplined. Father, by your grace, strengthen my will and make it move in your direction.

The one who calls you is faithful and he will do it (1 Thessalonians 5:24).
I know that nothing good lives in me, that is, in my sinful nature. For I have the desire to do what is good, but I cannot carry it out (Romans 7:18).
Let us examine our ways and test them, and let us return to the Lord (Lamentations 3:40).

Taking a Realistic View of Myself

People see me as a success in life, but I view myself as a failure in many important areas. It's sort of humorous to even talk about my *fear of failing* when I have failed so often. God, at times I have no confidence in anything I do or think.

I don't know what you intend to do to me or with me, but I know you knew me and saw this mess of my life long ago. You made the decision to love me and give yourself for me. I do trust you, but I must admit that I'm afraid of what is going to be necessary for me to do to become what you desire me to become.

I pray for the courage to live in truth, righteousness and justice during this time. Thank you for how you have provided for me during these last few years that I have been your son. I have an inner drive that desires to be channeled in the right way, but there is seemingly no place to direct it.

O Lord, you have searched me and you know me. You know when I sit and when I rise; you perceive my thoughts from afar. You discern my going out and my lying down; you are familiar with all my ways. Before a word is on my tongue you know it completely, O Lord. . . . For you created my inmost being; you knit me together in my mother's womb (Psalm 139:1-4,13). Show me your ways, O Lord, teach me your paths; guide me in your truth and teach me, for you are God my Savior, and my hope is in you all day long (Psalm 25:4,5).

FAITH

Taking God at His Word

Father, you tell me that I have received your Spirit by believing what I have heard. But how may I now live by believing what I hear? I do believe your Word, Father, when I act upon it, when I speak it and when I make decisions by it. I only deceive myself when I say I believe it but then don't act upon it.

You tell me to consider Abraham, to whom you simply gave a promise. His circumstances would indicate that there was no logical hope that your promise to him would ever come true. But he gave glory to you when he thanked you that you would do what you promised.

Father, give me the vision to live my life based simply upon your Word. When my emotions, my friends and my culture cry out to the contrary, give me the ability to stand on "Thus says the Lord."

Do not merely listen to the word, and so deceive yourselves. Do what it says. Anyone who listens to the word but does not do what it says is like a man who looks at his face in a mirror and, after looking at himself, goes away and immediately forgets what he looks like (James 1:22-24).

Without weakening in his faith, he faced the fact that his body was as good as dead—since he was about a hundred years old—and that Sarah's womb was also dead. Yet he did not waver through unbelief regarding the promise of God, but was strengthened in his faith and gave glory to God, being fully persuaded that God had power to do what he had promised (Romans 4:19-21).

Faith—Whatever the Odds

In Mark 2 where you heal the paralytic, Lord, you state that you saw their faith. To me that means you saw their *actions* of digging through the roof. If I am to live by faith, I must *act*. Many times this will mean to speak out, even though emotionally I may not wish to speak. At other times it will mean continuing onward with the same attitude Jonathan had when he said to his armorbearer, "Let us see what God will do." Then he and his armorbearer attacked the Philistine army, even though they were greatly outnumbered. When you are involved in one's life, it is certainly correct to have Jonathan's attitude which was, "It matters not with God whether there are many or few."

Father, I believe this is the correct attitude to have when you are in the center of one's belief—no matter what the odds.

But solid food is for the mature, who by constant use have trained themselves to distinguish good from evil (Hebrews 5:14).

What, then, shall we say in response to this? If God is for us, who can be against us? (Romans 8:31).

My Faith Does Waver

There are many principles in your Word which are to be believed. I desire to believe them, but sometimes I don't see the reality of the belief in my life. If I truly do believe your principles, why is there not more action in my life? Faith in your principles means I must trust those principles; and if I trust, then act upon them.

I have no problem believing that my sins are forgiven. But when you tell me that "I will dwell in them and walk among them," or, "Never will I leave you," or, "I will be with you always," my belief wavers. I hear those statements and want to believe them, but I don't see the joy and peace which should come as a result of building my life around the reality of those facts.

Help me, Father, live the reality of these statements rather than just hearing the words.

Therefore everyone who hears these words of mine and puts them into practice is like a wise man who built his house on the rock (Matthew 7:24).
And surely I will be with you always, to the very end of the age (Matthew 28:20).
Never will I leave you; never will I forsake you (Hebrews 13:5).

The Unseen—True Reality

My eyes substantiate the objects and colors in this room. If I close my eyes I cannot see the objects or the colors; but they are still there, for they are real. How do I know? When I open my eyes I see the reality of them.

My faith in Scripture likewise substantiates the reality of unseen facts to me. If it were the case that I didn't believe your Word, these unseen facts are real and factual just the same. But when I do believe them, faith opens my eyes to substantiate them.

"Live by faith"—faith means being *certain* of things we cannot see.

The men and women in Hebrews 11 lived by faith. Though all of your promises to them were eventually fulfilled, some of them died before seeing that fulfillment. Others lived to see the reality, but they believed *actively:* by faith Abraham *obeyed;* by faith Noah *constructed;* by faith Abraham *offered up* Isaac. They believed the promises to be true, so they acted. Lord, help me to act.

Now faith is being sure of what we hope for and certain of what we do not see (Hebrews 11:1).
As it is written: "The righteous will live by faith" (Romans 1:17).
We live by faith, not by sight (2 Corinthians 5:7).

Single-Minded Versus Double-Minded

I have been called *to live by faith.* If I am to live by faith I must focus on the unseen of what your Word says, rather than on the seen of my culture.

My platform for life must have the basic commitment of being pleasing to you, rather than being in bondage to the opinions of other men.

To do this I must be clearly single-minded with your ways, rather than being double-minded with my circumstances: "No one can serve two masters."

If I live by faith I will not only be a hearer, but a doer of Scripture. Paul said, "I believe; therefore, I have spoken." When I speak, I expose my faith.

Whoever claims to live in him must walk as Jesus did (1 John 2:6).
How on earth can you believe while you are for ever looking for one another's approval and not for the glory that comes from the one God? (John 5:44, Phillips).
Therefore, since we have such a hope, we are very bold (2 Corinthians 3:12).

When God Takes Us By Surprise

One of my problems of living by faith is to be able to accept as a fact the promise of oneness with Christ that His abiding presence brings to the Christian life. For example, I have a hard time accepting this with the proper attitude when it appears that you do not wish to use me in some particular way I expected. I expect you to use me in a great way; but when you don't, I ask myself, "Do these truths of the Word really work?" and I become discouraged in believing them.

The statutes you have laid down are righteous; they are fully trustworthy (Psalm 119:138).
"For my thoughts are not your thoughts, neither are your ways my ways," declares the Lord (Isaiah 55:8).

FAITHFULNESS

Being Well-Pleased

I have just finished speaking to a group of young people. My tendency is to think that you are well-pleased and I am blessed of you only if there is a great audience response when I share your Word. I tend to feel just the opposite if I give the same message and see no response; then I feel you are displeased with me or you are not using me.

This is a misconception on my part. Your desire is that we be faithful men and women who find their pleasure in simply being faithful to you, for you deserve our faithfulness. You are always more committed to me than I am to you.

Whoever can be trusted with very little can also be trusted with much, and whoever is dishonest with very little will also be dishonest with much (Luke 16:10).
Let every man learn to assess properly the value of his own work and he can then be glad when he has done something worth doing without depending on the approval of others (Galatians 6:4, Phillips).

Being Used in Spite of Myself

Lord, I've had no personal time with you in several days and my soul seems heavily burdened today.

It is good to know how your faithfulness takes over in situations where your truth needs to be spoken, even though I am disturbed and heavy in my spirit. Thank you for allowing me to meet that person's need to hear the gospel even when I seemed distant from your fellowship.

Your faithfulness continues through all generations; you established the earth, and it endures (Psalm 119:90).
But if I say, "I will not mention him or speak any more in his name," his word is in my heart like a burning fire, shut up in my bones. I am weary of holding it in; indeed, I cannot (Jeremiah 20:9).

When I Don't Want to Talk to God

There is a strong sensing of your presence with me today Lord, but I don't have a desire to talk with you. I feel discouraged that my life is not pleasing to you, though you never waver in your faithfulness. "If we are faithless, he will remain faithful."

You know when I sit and when I rise; you perceive my thoughts from afar. . . . You hem me in, behind and before; you have laid your hand upon me. . . . Where can I go from your Spirit? Where can I flee from your presence? (Psalm 139:2,5,7).
Remember not the sins of my youth and my rebellious ways; according to your love remember me, for you are good, O Lord (Psalm 25:7).

FEAR

My Fear of Failure

Why do I fear to act in the unknown? Is it because I don't want to fail? Why do I fear failure so much? It must be a deeper fear of rejection. In my pride and haughtiness I am indicating that I am the one responsible for my success.

I shouldn't fear the unknown, for as a Christian I know the One who alone controls the unknown.

Even though I walk through the valley of the shadow of death, I will fear no evil, for you are with me; your rod and your staff, they comfort me (Psalm 23:4).

You will not fear the terror of night, nor the arrow that flies by day, nor the pestilence that stalks in the darkness, nor the plague that destroys at midday. . . . If you make the Most High your dwelling—even the Lord, who is my refuge—then no harm will befall you (Psalm 91:5,6, 9,10).

FOCUS

Anger, the Wrong Focus

Lord, my anger toward a certain person today has caused me to complain and find fault with your ways toward me. Why do I focus on the person instead of on your scriptural principles of love, kindness and forgiveness? If only I would obey these principles, you would be free to allow your spirit to bring your blessings to my life.

Try me and know my ways, Father. See what evil is in me, then please deal with that evil in your abundant grace.

Search me, O God, and know my heart; test me and know my anxious thoughts. See if there is any offensive way in me, and lead me in the way everlasting (Psalms 139:23,24).
And the Lord's servant must not quarrel; instead, he must be kind to everyone, able to teach, not resentful (2 Timothy 2:24).
Do everything without complaining or arguing (Philippians 2:14).

Making Sure the Focus Is Right

I am so concerned with how much I love others and with how faithful to you I am that I become defeated when I fall short. If I could simply learn to focus on all you say you will do, then my faithfulness would be as a result of my excitement over your faithfulness!

Let me understand the teaching of your precepts; then I will meditate on your wonders (Psalm 119:27).
If we are faithless, he will remain faithful, for he cannot disown himself (2 Timothy 2:13).
Find rest, O my soul, in God alone; my hope comes from him (Psalm 62:5).

Hindrances to One's Effectiveness

The key hindrances to one's life according to Mark 10 are:
1. Cares of the world
2. Deceitfulness of riches
3. Desire for others' things
4. Glory of men.

The cares of the world can only be dealt with as I cast these cares upon you and choose to carry other men's cares.

The deceitfulness of riches must be put in the grave that allows one to seek first your Kingdom.

The desire for other things must be seen as pennies, compared to nuggets of gold as I obey the command to seek those things that are above.

The glory of men must be laid aside for the approval and applause of God.

But the worries of this life, the deceitfulness of wealth and the desires for other things come in and choke the word, making it unfruitful (Mark 4:19).
Am I now trying to win the approval of men, or of God? Or am I trying to please men? If I were still trying to please men, I would not be a servant of Christ (Galatians 1:10).
Set your minds on things above, not on earthly things (Colossians 3:2).

When I Seem to Have Little to Offer

My self-confidence is very low today, but maybe this is where you want me, Father. At times, I have no confidence in my ability to think or speak in logical thought patterns. Sometimes I wonder if I have any common sense at all!

Father, my confidence is in your Spirit's working out your thoughts and ways through my mind. There I have no doubts. Lord, I present my mind to you. You tell me in Proverbs to commit my way to you, and so shall my thoughts be developed.

Allow me to think and see as you do today, Father.

But we have the mind of Christ (1 Corinthians 2:16).
Brothers, think of what you were when you were called. Not many of you were wise by human standards; not many were influential; not many were of noble birth. But God chose the foolish things of the world to shame the wise; God chose the weak things of the world to shame the strong. He chose the lowly things of this world and the despised things—and the things that are not—to nullify the things that are, so that no one may boast before him (1 Corinthians 1:26-29).

FORGIVENESS

When I Break My Father's Heart

Father, because of Him who said, "Shall I not drink the cup the Father has given me," I can come by means of His blood to your throne of grace, a throne which is for those in time of need. My confession of those areas of my life which have been displeasing to you is made with the security that you accept me in Christ.

My lack of faith has grieved you much this week. As always, my unbelief has grown into pride in wanting what I thought was best and not what others thought best. Forgive me for the many times I have focused the conversation on me for selfish and insecure reasons and for the times I took credit for that which did not belong to me.

Forgive me for the times this week when I have used the word "I" instead of "we"; I wanted to promote myself instead of others. I have resented certain people, but the real problem has been my own rebellion to your ways. Instead of acknowledging my inabilities and inadequacies, which would have caused me to depend upon you more, I have been a pretense. Forgive me.

Teach me as you taught Paul—to glory in my weakness. Thank you that the debt of all of these inadequacies has been paid by my Saviour. I claim your forgiveness.

Blessed are they whose transgressions are forgiven, whose sins are covered. Blessed is the man whose sin the Lord will never count against him (Romans 4:7,8).
For we do not have a high priest who is unable to sympathize with our weaknesses, but we have one who has been tempted in every way, just as we are—yet was without sin. Let us then approach the throne of grace with confidence, so that we may receive mercy and find grace to help us in our time of need (Hebrews 4:15,16).

GOD'S WILL

God's Way Versus Job Security

I'm going through an aftermath of emotion, for I just discussed with my partner the possibility of moving our company to another part of the country—and his moving with the company. I must see your hand in this and try to see your desire. Help me trust you even if what you want seems to be contrary to my desire. Let me not fear change or so-called job "security." Let my desire be toward you alone while I'm on this earth. Let me decide in this situation based on what is best for others and not me alone. Keep my hurt and misunderstanding pure so you will be free to work in me that which will give you honor and glory.

And David behaved himself wisely in all his ways; and the Lord was with him (1 Samuel 18:14, KJV).
I am still confident of this: I will see the goodness of the Lord in the land of the living. Wait for the Lord; be strong and take heart and wait for the Lord (Psalm 27:13,14).

HOLINESS

Developing a Cutting Edge

Lord, I feel that my outward life should manifest to unbelievers that I am yours. Jesus has called me to holiness in every area of living. If Jesus were to come back today, what areas of my life would I feel convicted about—that never got in order because I had the attitude of, "I'll get it done one day"?

I seem to find time for everything I think is important in my business and my recreational life, but tend to put off those areas that need attention to your conformity. Help me to realize that conformity to your likeness needs to be my most urgent matter in this life.

Who can discern his errors? Forgive my hidden faults. Keep your servant also from willful sins; may they not rule over me (Psalm 19:12,13).
So we make it our goal to please him, whether we are at home in the body or away from it (2 Corinthians 5:9).

HOLY SPIRIT

Freedom Through Dependence

To live and walk by means of the Holy Spirit is to trust the Spirit to do in me and for me what I cannot do myself. As I trust a doctor to do for me what I cannot do myself and as I trust a lawyer to do for me what I cannot do myself, so must I be dependent upon the Holy Spirit. expectant that He will fulfill the responsibilities entrusted to Him in the same way as a faithful doctor or lawyer would. As I must be obedient to the doctor or lawyer I have entrusted myself to, so must I be obedient to the leadership of the Holy Spirit.

With this frame of reference of obedience to the One to whom the responsibilities of life have been entrusted, I dare not say, "I cannot" at the command He gives me.

But when he, the Spirit of truth, comes, he will guide you into all truth. He will not speak on his own; he will speak only what he hears, and he will tell you what is yet to come (John 16:13).
So I say, live by the Spirit, and you will not gratify the desires of the sinful nature (Galatians 5:16).
I can do everything through him who gives me strength (Philippians 4:13).

HOME

The Laboratory of Love

The primary place where love is learned is in the home. Love is learned and experienced here *first*. In the home there are relationships which are primarily designed with the motive of giving instead of getting. In the home most pretense has been removed and the real you is exposed. There is no acclaim or applause in the home for some of those things that we do in public when we try to be something we are not. Lord, this is your laboratory for change that is lasting.

And we, who with unveiled faces all reflect the Lord's glory, are being transformed into his likeness with ever-increasing glory, which comes from the Lord, who is the Spirit (2 Corinthians 3:18).

HONESTY

A Godly Epitaph

At the end when Samuel was retiring as the prophet of God, his overview of life was:

whose oxen have I taken,
whose donkey have I taken,
whom have I defrauded,
whom have I oppressed,
whom have I bribed?

The people he served responded that he had not taken anything from any man's hand. Father, if I were to ask why you used this man and gave him special abilities, I believe your answer would be that he did not use them for his own gains. I pray for these qualities in my daily life as I do business in my culture.

Better the little that the righteous have than the wealth of the many wicked (Psalm 37:16).
Since an overseer is entrusted with God's work, he must be blameless . . . not pursuing dishonest gain (Titus 1:7).

INFLUENCE

Do I Want Out?

I am getting tired of calling on people in business for the purpose of getting something from them by selling to them. It is a great temptation to sell the company to be free only to give to people and not to get. Lord, please allow me to focus on you and trust your way. Help me be free with you in regard to getting the orders or not getting the orders.

Let the *needs* of the people I relate to have priority over "making the sale." Let me communicate a spirit of genuineness to them whether they do business with me or not. My company will have little value 100 years from now, but my availability to your Spirit in behalf of others has true lasting value.

I try to please everybody in every way. For I am not seeking my own good but the good of many, so that they may be saved (1 Corinthians 10:33).

KNOWING GOD

Understanding Who God Is

Lord, these words which describe you in the Psalms were written by a man who earnestly desired your desires, the man David:

The Lord is my *shepherd,*
   the Lord is my *salvation,*
      the Lord is my *strength,*
         the Lord is my *fortress,*
            the Lord is my *high tower,*
               the Lord is *my hope.*

Help me desire you as David did. Help me understand my life in light of who you are and what you wish to be to me. Also allow me to understand that these desires flow from the following statements of David which deal with your character:

"The Lord is gracious and compassionate" (111:4).

"The works of His hands are faithful and just" (111:7).

"Righteousness and justice are the foundation of your throne" (89:14).

"Love and faithfulness go before you" (89:14).

He wraps himself in light as with a garment" (104:2).

But let him who boasts boast about this: that he understands and knows me, that I am the Lord, who exercises kindness, justice and righteousness on earth, for in these I delight (Jeremiah 9:24).

Does he speak and then not act? Does he promise and then not fulfill? (Numbers 23:19).

LABOR

Activity in Vain

Paul wanted to be able to boast to you that he did not labor in vain. I have labored some for you, Father, but I fear that much of my activity for you has been in vain. I fear that not too much of my fruit will last because my motives were often those of selfish ambition. We, as believers, know that only that which involves the cause of the Kingdom will have lasting value. It is disaster for us to waste our lives.

However, Father, even with all my weaknesses and blind spots, I have a deep desire to be used by you for your glory. I do hope that much of what I have gone through is part of a preparation for a ministry that *will* be fruitful for you before I come home to be with you.

May my life be well pleasing in your sight and joyous to your heart today.

. . .in order that I may boast on the day of Christ that I did not run or labor for nothing (Philippians 2:16).

LOVE

Walking in Someone Else's Shoes

The principle of love is the life of faith.

Your Word tells me, "Nobody should seek his own good, but the good of others," and that I am to "look not only to your own interests, but also to the interests of others." You also tell me to "learn to see things from other people's point of view." These admonishments are the foundation of the life of love, which, if carried out, become the walk of faith because they contradict everything that culture and our society says.

You say to walk by faith. If I do, my footsteps will be those that are grounded in the principles of love. The world wants power to control, and many times when I pray for power for my Christian life I am afraid that my motive is the same as that of the world. When I understand that your power in my life is the power to produce meekness, gentleness, patience and forbearance, I realize that this is a power which endows me to love the way you love.

None of you should think only of his own affairs, but each should learn to see things from other people's point of view (Philippians 2:4, Phillips).
Nobody should seek his own good, but the good of others (1 Corinthians 10:24).

How to Love the Unlovely

At times, love at the feeling level must come from choosing to act as if you love those you don't think you ever could love. The emotion of love comes when this happens.

Do everything in love (1 Corinthians 16:14).
Do not merely listen to the word, and so deceive yourselves.
Do what it says (James 1:22).

The Ultimate Aim

Since your Word says that the ultimate aim of the Christian life is to produce love, then my whole existence as a Christian is to be rooted and grounded in love. This love can only flow from a pure heart (one that seeks no personal gain), a clear conscience (one that makes me void of offense toward man and God) and genuine faith (a trust in your ways).

Father, teach me what it means to have "the love of Christ control" me. Thank you for saying "love never fails"—but please help me to act upon that truth by faith in my interpersonal relationships with people. Teach me the joy of your reality which says that those who lose their lives (by following the principles of love) will find their lives. Place me within the truth which says though I would have all knowledge, all faith, excellence in speaking and the greatest in giving, I accomplish *absolutely nothing* if I do not love.

Lord Jesus, the action of your life reflects the supreme example of the life of love. You came not to please yourself; not to be served, but to serve; and not to be ministered to, but to minister. Your supreme example was when you laid down your life for me and the world.

For in Christ Jesus neither circumcision nor uncircumcision has any value. The only thing that counts is faith expressing itself through love (Galatians 5:6).
For whoever wants to save his life will lose it, but whoever loses his life for me will save it (Luke 9:24).

Do I Carry Others' Burdens?

Father, you tell me that I have been made free—free to serve others in love. You explain the how-to of doing this by the principle which says I should cast my personal burdens on you, but also to carry the burdens of those around me by assuming personal responsibility for them. If I walk by faith in you, I must live by faith in the principle of love. To live by love is to walk by faith.

It is interesting that a focus of New Testament Christianity was based upon Christians' selling all they had to help meet each other's needs. If I refuse to operate on the principle of "that which is best for the other person," I may subconsciously not expect you to do that which is best for me, even though you will always seek my best no matter what my unbelief. But if my focus is on others, I free myself to your power and to your active involvement on my behalf.

Cast all your anxiety on him because he cares for you
(1 Peter 5:7).
You, my brothers, were called to be free. But do not use your
freedom to indulge the sinful nature; rather, serve one another
in love (Galatians 5:13).
Carry each other's burdens, and in this way you will fulfill the
law of Christ (Galatians 6:2).

Learning to Love in Leadership

Lord, my basic need is to love.

But it seems to be difficult for me to learn the true meaning of biblical love because I am usually in the dominant or leadership position with people. I'm responsible to accomplish certain goals, and when I feel pressure developing that I may not meet those goals I tend to react insensitively to those around me.

My leadership relationship with my wife also tests my true motives. This shows me that my love, at times, is not sufficiently sensitive. Again, this insensitivity comes from the wrong response to pressure. Until I can experience the true meaning of love and sensitivity with my wife I won't know much about loving others.

A new commandment I give you: Love one another. As I have loved you, so you must love one another. All men will know that you are my disciples if you love one another (John 13:34,35).

He does not treat us as our sins deserve or repay us according to our iniquities. For as high as the heavens are above the earth, so great is his love for those who fear him; as far as the east is from the west, so far has he removed our transgressions from us (Psalm 103:10-12).

MEDITATION

The Road to Preparation

I can truly see the importance of meditation on your Word. When I am in the midst of fleshly conflict those principles which I have meditated on are brought to my attention by the Holy Spirit who motivates my soul and mind to be obedient. I believe Joseph had many times mulled over in his mind your point of view as to the proper response to take even before Potiphar's wife made sexual advances toward him. He was not caught by surprise.

Do not let this Book of the Law depart from your mouth; meditate on it day and night, so that you may be careful to do everything written in it. Then you will be prosperous and successful (Joshua 1:8).
How can a young man keep his way pure? By living according to your word. I seek you with all my heart; do not let me stray from your commands. I have hidden your word in my heart that I might not sin against you (Psalm 119:9-11).
I meditate on your precepts and consider your ways (Psalm 119:15).

When Everything Else Takes His Place

It is amazing how many things come into my life which interfere with my time with you. In order to be able to speak and live by your Spirit, I must rearrange my priorities to be able to spend time with you, the source of all my strength.

Though princes sit together and slander me, your servant will meditate on your decrees (Psalm 119:23).
Oh, how I love your law! I meditate on it all day long. I have more insight than all my teachers, for I meditate on your statutes (Psalm 119:97,99).

MEEKNESS
All of Life Is a Gift

Why do I have a job . . .
Why do I have food . . .
Why do I have clothes . . .
Why do I have health . . .
Why do I have purpose and destiny . . .

. . . when so many others don't? The only answer is for me to bow before you and praise you for your graciousness toward me. True meekness can only come in realizing that all life is a gift and that you are the sovereign Lord and King. And you can do as you please with me and anyone else.

What is man that you are mindful of him, the son of man that you care for him? (Psalm 8:4).
For who makes you different from anyone else? What do you have that you did not receive? And if you did receive it, why do you boast as though you did not? (1 Corinthians 4:7).

God's True Gift—Life!

My very present moment of existence is but a gift given to me by you, Father. My next life's breath is your gift. Understanding this, my perspective and decisions in life should be built around the commitment to build your Kingdom and not my own kingdom. As a result of being alive only by your permission, let my heart's desire be only to bring glory to you and to find my good pleasure in your will alone.

Father, send your Spirit mightily upon me to accomplish this.

Why, you do not even know what will happen tomorrow. What is your life? You are a mist that appears for a little while and then vanishes. Instead, you ought to say, "If it is the Lord's will, we will live and do this or that" (James 4:14,15).

Show me, O Lord, my life's end and the number of my days; let me know how fleeting is my life (Psalm 39:4).

MONEY

The Root of Many Evils

Jesus, you said that man cannot serve God and money. I need to make a basic decision in my life regarding my attitude toward these two issues. It is interesting to note that, of all things, you choose to separate yourself and money. I cannot be loyal to both. I must have a correct balance between the two. When I compromise, selfish gain is usually the root.

You tested Abraham by asking him to offer Isaac, his son. Then, because he had not withheld from you that which he most loved, you gave it back to him. Do I love money? May I offer "money" and all it stands for in my past, present and future to you as Abraham offered his only son?

For the love of money is a root of all kinds of evil. Some people, eager for money, have wandered from the faith and pierced themselves with many griefs (1 Timothy 6:10).

Mixing Money and Friendship

I am in California this week to see if I should get involved with a certain company. Even though a clear understanding has been given in regard to all business agreements, my fear is that my friendship relationship with the people of this company will become hampered because of the financial arrangements. The agreement, though fair, may tempt some to desire more money once the company is turned around. I have often seen Christian brothers split over "surface" issues, when the real reason was *money*.

God, protect me from the "dollar" and my own selfishness. Much of this reaction may be due to my personal hang-ups which I am projecting onto others. Your statement that I cannot serve both you and money certainly makes the issue clear.

Whoever loves money never has money enough; whoever loves wealth is never satisfied with his income. This too is meaningless (Ecclesiastes 5:10).

MOTIVATION

Determining True Meaning and Purpose

After a day's work, I need to ask myself what has purpose outside of you. If I am commanded to do *all* for your glory and to do *all* in your name, there seems to be only lasting meaning if this principle is applied to each experience and circumstance.

As I evaluate many things I have done in the past as to where they will stand in eternity, I see much of my life going up in the smoke of wood, hay and stubble. It isn't that the things themselves were necessarily meaningless, but it was because my motivation was wrong. I did them for *my* glory and in *my* name: the thrill of the football field; a successful business deal; a selfish relationship with a person. If only my attitude had been one of dependence upon you!

I have fed my ego with fame, honor, attention, the desire to be recognized, the desire to be well-spoken of and with seeking praise for my athletic and professional skills—all of which, today, have no lasting value.

Father, I utter the words of the psalmist, "Show me, O Lord, my life's end and the number of my days; let me know how fleeting is my life." I am involved in the same struggles of life now as before; the difference is that I have another frame of reference now. Help me to believe and apply in all my activities the words of Jesus: "Apart from me you can do nothing."

So whether you eat or drink or whatever you do, do it all for the glory of God (1 Corinthians 10:31).
And whatever you do, whether in word or deed, do it all in the name of the Lord Jesus, giving thanks to God the Father through him (Colossians 3:17).

Whose Approval Do I Seek?

How different the life-style of your man should be from that of the culture he lives in! You tell me not to be "ambitious of my own reputation," while the market-place is built on men promoting their own reputation. The proper motivation is to do my work without desiring the approval of others. I should desire your approval first.

As I do my work unto you, I am motivated to do my very best; and if my best is accomplished according to your standards, then that alone makes me glad and will build self-worth without depending upon the approval of others.

Let us not be ambitious for our own reputations, for that only means making one another jealous (Galatians 5:26, Phillips).

Understanding Myself for Others' Sake

The inward motivation to reach out to others is basic. But we must also learn to focus on ourselves and who and what we are so we can give to others more intelligently. If I am focusing on what the other thinks or how I can impress or conquer him, I do not have the attitude that will allow your Holy Spirit to function in freedom to reproduce your life and fruits. If my attitude is that of helping meet the needs of those around me, then you are free to work your life in and through me. You never fill us with your Spirit for our selfish gain.

Unless the Lord builds the house, its builders labor in vain (Psalm 127:1).
But when he, the Spirit of truth, comes, he will guide you into all truth (John 16:13).
Send forth your light and your truth, let them guide me; let them bring me to your holy mountain, to the place where you dwell (Psalm 43:3).

Understanding the Fear of the Lord

While going to work today, I was traveling 70 mph in a 50 mph zone. I was free from conviction until I saw a policeman. I slowed down to 50 mph when I saw the representative of the law who has the power to enforce the law and bring me under a penalty.

I think, Father, this is illustrative of the reality of living in your presence and shows the true meaning of "the fear of the Lord is the beginning of knowledge." As I live in the presence of the standard of Jesus, it is as driving in the presence of the policeman. This shows the importance of having Christ at the center of every attitude and action. When I see a police car, I am motivated to do right because of fear of punishment. With Christ in my presence, I am motivated to do right because of love for Him who took my punishment for all my sins on the cross, including going 70 mph in a 50 mph zone.

The fear of the Lord is the beginning of knowledge, but fools despise wisdom and discipline (Proverbs 1:7).
Then the church throughout Judea, Galilee and Samaria enjoyed a time of peace. It was strengthened; and encouraged by the Holy Spirit, it grew in numbers, living in the fear of the Lord (Acts 9:31).
This is love for God: to obey his commands. And his commands are not burdensome (1 John 5:3).

MOTIVES

Shame That Leads to Glory

Jesus was faced with a decision: He could have the glory and splendor of the world offered by Satan or He could face the shame of the cross offered by you, Father.

I must be careful, Lord, in thinking that because I am serving you, you will shower me with material blessings. My heart will then deceive me into choosing your way because the end result will be earthly rewards. That is not the correct motive.

The correct motive is that I should serve you simply because it is your desire and it brings glory to your name—not from the belief I will get something.

Jesus chose the right course and had the right response to each situation, but all He received in His life on earth was rejection, suffering, shame and crucifixion.

Though the fig tree does not bud and there are no grapes on the vines, though the olive crop fails and the fields produce no food, though there are no sheep in the pen and no cattle in the stalls, yet I will rejoice in the Lord, I will be joyful in God my Savior. The Sovereign Lord is my strength; he makes my feet like the feet of a deer, he enables me to go on the heights (Habakkuk 3:17-19).

Growth in Having Proper Motives

As a Christian businessman I see that most of my business relationships are based upon the answer to: "What will I lose or gain by doing this or that?" How does this all fit into my being guided by the principles of love?

The right question for me to focus on is what will my client gain if I do this or what will he lose if I don't. That is the way of love, and you have promised me that "love never fails."

This love of which I speak is slow to lose patience—it looks for a way of being constructive. It is not possessive: it is neither anxious to impress nor does it cherish inflated ideas of its own importance. Love has good manners and does not pursue selfish advantage. It is not touchy. It does not keep account of evil or gloat over the wickedness of other people. On the contrary, it is glad with all good men when truth prevails. Love knows no limit to its endurance, no end to its trust, no fading of its hope; it can outlast anything (1 Corinthians 13:4-7, Phillips).

My Creativeness in Rationalizing

It is annoying how the human heart can justify selfish motives in such a way as to think we are giving instead of taking. Father, it seems that my heart can rationalize so easily—even to the point that I think I am doing something for you when my desire may be for personal gain. You alone can save me from myself.

The heart is deceitful above all things and beyond cure. Who can understand it? (Jeremiah 17:9).
All a man's ways seem innocent to him, but motives are weighed by the Lord (Proverbs 16:2).

My Life on Your Stage

My work unto you is contrary to all that my culture says and my eyes experience. My work must be activated in my life by faith alone. I must see clearly that I am on a stage, your stage, and that my goal should be to receive your applause and praise in eternity. I need to realize that the praise of men lasts only a few moments.

I think it is interesting, Father, to know that you say you shall bring to light the secret motives of men's hearts and *then* you will give each man his share of praise. Teach me to stay in your light so my motives will be clear and so my life will be lived in your presence for your approval.

When the Lord comes he will bring into the light of day all that at present is hidden in darkness, and he will expose the secret motives of men's hearts. Then shall God himself give each man his share of praise (1 Corinthians 4:5, Phillips).

The Key to Walking in Light and Love

To have your life as my source of strength, I must have your motives as my motives. This is the key to walking in the light and in love. Light makes my motives clear; love examines whether they are correct or incorrect.

In many social and business relationships, whether with men or women, our motives are often those of control, sex, praise, impressiveness, money, power, etc. Only by means of your life being lived in me can my natural tendencies be changed to give me all that flows from your life, which frame of reference is love. Such a quality of life causes me to be motivated to move in behalf of others without any desire for selfish gain.

Greater love has no one than this, that one lay down his life for his friends (John 15:13).

The True Motive for Serving

My serving others is a ministry for you.

But I have a problem in this regard. I feel more pleased when I serve you publicly and that ministry is blessed than I do when there is no public acclaim, such as caring for my wife when she is ill.

Lord, purify my motives!

Am I living my life for you or for the praise of man?

Why do I not desire to be a street cleaner, waiter, short-order cook or telephone operator? Is it because there isn't the same esteem in the eyes of the public as my job gives? I know you only regard the man's heart, not how he makes his livelihood.

Do I want people to think well of me because I am serving you? If they didn't, what then would be my motive for serving you? Would I even want to serve you? These are serious questions about my spiritual life I must face.

You highly esteem a meek and quiet spirit, regardless of the type of work a person does. Help me to make decisions based upon your value system.

The King will reply, "I tell you the truth, whatever you did for one of the least of these brothers of mine, you did for me" (Matthew 25:40).
But when you pray, do not be like the hypocrites, for they love to pray standing in the synagogues and on the street corners to be seen by men. I tell you the truth, they have received their reward in full (Matthew 6:5).

OPENNESS

We All Wear a Mask

Lord, what silly, stupid games we play—our hearts crying out for fulfillment!

Two men are sitting at a table with a girl and are talking about hunting. One says, "I hunt this way." The other says, "I hunt that way." The girl smiles politely and thinks, *What a stupid conversation,* but is fearful to say what she really thinks because she too wants to be accepted.

The men are pleased with her because she smiles pleasantly as they talk about what they enjoy.

Each one wears a mask! One of them is me. In essence this is lying.

Lord, help me be more honest and sensitive to the interests of others.

Let us therefore make every effort to do what leads to peace and to mutual edification (Romans 14:19).
None of you should think only of his own affairs, but each should learn to see things from other people's point of view (Philippians 2:4, Phillips).
Help, Lord, for the godly are no more; the faithful have vanished from among men. Everyone lies to his neighbor; their flattering lips speak with deception (Psalm 12:1,2).

OPPORTUNITY

Whose Kingdom Am I Building?

Lord, man must have a mission, a goal and a mark that will last more than his 70 years. My life must be governed by decisions that will last and have meaning 100 years from now. To live with this mentality I need to see my life on planet earth as that of a stranger passing through, as a citizen of another world.

My motivation as a man in business must not be for my own glory, but for yours. It must not be a life that is to please me, but one that pleases you; "not my will, but your will" be done.

Time is short; therefore, I must buy up the opportunities.

Jesus said, "To this end was I born." Father, what is my end? What is my mandate?

[You] are not of this world, any more than I am of the world (John 17:14).
Be very careful, then, how you live . . . making the most of every opportunity, because the days are evil (Ephesians 5:16).
Be wise in the way you act toward outsiders; make the most of every opportunity (Colossians 4:5).

OVERCOMING

When I Reject His Best

There seems to be a real unwillingness to carry out what you have taught me, Father. Every time I sin in a way in which I am deeply grieved, my sorrow is from the fact that you have demonstrated yourself so clearly in the situation. My sorrow is for the overt rejection of your will, which I know to be for my good—instead I opted for the momentary satisfaction of my selfishness and its lust. Thank you for your faithfulness in pointing out these areas in my life, for my confidence today is in your Son for my victory and your glory.

You, dear children, are from God and have overcome them, because the one who is in you is greater than the one who is in the world (1 John 4:4).
For everyone born of God has overcome the world. This is the victory that has overcome the world, even our faith (1 John 5:4).

PATIENCE

False Expectations of God

I tend to think you should instantaneously respond whenever I eagerly believe something by faith. This is a misconception. Rather, you desire me not to focus on *how* or *when* you will do a thing, but that you *will* do it.

Christian maturity is reflected by the length of time I am willing to wait for you to respond the way you have promised after I have entered into believing faith on some particular matter. It is the length of time I am willing to wait between achievement and reward that determines my maturity.

You need to persevere so that when you have done the will of God, you will receive what he has promised (Hebrews 10:36). And so after waiting patiently, Abraham received what was promised (Hebrews 6:15).

PEACE

When I Am Truly Bearing Fruit

Lord, you said you would give peace.

When I am experiencing it, I sometimes tend to think it isn't really a fruit of your Spirit unless other people sense it in me and talk about it.

Thank you for showing me that inner fruit is unto you. If the inward experience is right, you *are* being glorified— even if those around me are unaware of my peace and joy.

So whether you eat or drink or whatever you do, do it all for the glory of God (1 Corinthians 10:31).
Peace I leave with you; my peace I give you. I do not give to you as the world gives. Do not let your hearts be troubled and do not be afraid (John 14:27).
I have told you these things, so that in me you may have peace. In this world you will have trouble. But take heart! I have overcome the world (John 16:33).

PLANNING

When Improper Feelings Precede Planning

Lord, I truly desire to do something beneficial for the people in my company. However, I see a tendency in my planning often to overlook some of the necessities, which makes me improperly prepared for the entire situation. Few things ever work out the way I have planned them on paper. Maybe too much of my motivation is greed rather than trying to benefit others.

Heavenly Father, I trust the ideas I have for the company are from you. Help me not to force anything by allowing my emotions to run too far ahead of realistic planning. I pray that I will do things your way and simply trust you the way you want me to trust you.

Not slothful in business; fervent in spirit; serving the Lord (Romans 12:11, KJV).
With your help I can advance against a troop; with my God I can scale a wall (Psalm 18:29).

PLEASING GOD

Presumptions About Others' Thoughts

As I was looking in the rearview mirror of my car at a Christian brother I had just left, I began to feel anxious about what I was thinking in regard to what I thought he must be thinking about me. Many times my lack of self-acceptance comes from an imaginary problem I create. It is when I think someone else is thinking something about me, when actually, most of the time they haven't thought what I thought they thought.

Lord, as these emotions develop, help me turn my thoughts to you and evaluate my behavior in your presence. Help me not to think about what others may be thinking about me, which really shows my egotism. Instead, help me think what *you* are thinking about me. This gives me a sense of the freedom you desire me to have in interpersonal relationships.

How precious to me are your thoughts, O God! How vast is the sum of them! Were I to count them, they would outnumber the grains of sand. When I awake, I am still with you (Psalm 139:17,18).
May the words of my mouth and the meditation of my heart be pleasing in your sight, O Lord, my Rock and my Redeemer (Psalm 19:14).

POSSESSIONS

When I Call God a Liar

I have a spirit of rebellion in me that makes me think you owe me something. I'm often available to you, Lord, when everything is going well and my fears have been satisfied by spiritual success. But when you bring pressure on me, I am ready to toss everything overboard.

Forgive me, Father, for my resentment and complaining spirit that, in essence, is calling you a liar. What I am within myself is wretched. Thank you for saving me from myself and sin and drawing me to yourself for eternity. I have no hope outside of your marvelous grace toward me. My usefulness is dependent upon your fruit in me.

This has been a good time with you, Lord. Thanks for also helping me to remember that the money I have been entrusted with is yours, and you are free to give or to take it away. I thank you that the ownership of my possessions has now been given back to you. Now my only possession is the Lord Jesus.

Naked I came from my mother's womb, and naked I will depart. The Lord gave and the Lord has taken away; may the name of the Lord be praised (Job 1:21).
But whatever was to my profit I now consider loss for the sake of Christ. What is more, I consider everything a loss compared to the surpassing greatness of knowing Christ Jesus my Lord, for whose sake I have lost all things. I consider them rubbish, that I may gain Christ (Philippians 3:7,8).

POWER

The Exhausting Christian Life

Some of us tend to drive ourselves too hard by sheer willpower, then say that the Christian life is an exhausting and bitter one. We have forced ourselves to be something we are not.

I guess, Father, the reason I think I can please you with willpower is because I still tend to think that I can perform in the spiritual world with *my abilities* instead of accepting your words, "Apart from me you can do nothing."

Willpower may be acceptable in the business community, but it is only the will yielded to your power that will be accepted in the halls of heaven.

I can do everything through him who gives me strength (Philippians 4:13).
I am the vine; you are the branches. If a man remains in me and I in him, he will bear much fruit; apart from me you can do nothing (John 15:5).
This is the word of the Lord to Zerubbabel: "Not by might nor by power, but by my Spirit," says the Lord Almighty (Zechariah 4:6).

True Power Equals Meekness

We desire power to be able to get what we want. We think of the power to rule over people, power of money and power of control. You say we have received your power to be a witness. The power you desire me to be strengthened with is a power that will allow me to apply meekness instead of arrogance, humility instead of pride, patience instead of impatience, love instead of bitterness. God, the power you want me to have is your life of grace in behalf of others flowing through me, one of your people.

Being strengthened with all power according to his glorious might so that you may have great endurance and patience (Colossians 1:11).

Faith + Love = Power

Three key words in the New Testament: faith, love and power. I don't think power will be given or manifested in the believer's life unless his motivation is that of love applied by the attitude of faith. Jesus never used His power for Himself, but always for others. This demonstrates the basic goal of the Christian life: to love. This truly is the secret of a man's own heart before you, but the power (which we are probably not even aware of) will be visible through impact to other people in the form of love.

A formula: *faith* (the attitude that the principle of love is the key to life in giving or receiving) + *love* (the inward motive and desire to meet the needs of others with no desire for personal gain) = *power* (the outworking of the presence of Christ being manifested in and through our thoughts, words and deeds).

Conclusion: Your glory for changing the heart of man through grace.

For God did not give us a spirit of timidity, but a spirit of power, of love and of self-discipline (2 Timothy 1:7).
But you will receive power when the Holy Spirit comes on you; and you will be my witnesses in Jerusalem, and in all Judea and Samaria, and to the ends of the earth (Acts 1:8).

Acting Like His Son

You say that if I have received your Son, you will give me the power to be and act like your Son. Understanding this, I must realize that at this moment you are energizing me to act like your Son and are enabling me to do what I ought.

To be able for me to do this, there must be a discipline of mind and a concentration on the right attitudes so that I will heed the prompting of your Spirit to act according to your will.

In every cause and effect relationship there needs to be that inward focus on Jesus.

Yet to all who received him, to those who believed in his name, he gave the right to become children of God (John 1:12).
For it is God who is at work within you, giving you the will and the power to achieve his purpose (Philippians 2:13, Phillips).

Two Views—God's and Mine

Father, I fear that my concept of power and your concept of giving me power are two different things at times.

It is noteworthy to see that Jesus had all the power of the Godhead at His command. Jesus wanted to communicate truth, but only in the context of "learn from me, for I am gentle and humble in heart." He made no reputation for Himself, and His freedom from the opinions of people came from desiring not the approval of men, but the approval of you, His Father. His criteria for being with people was not to be served, but to serve and to give His life as a ransom.

Reflecting all of this against many of my desires for power, I see my motive has often been to build a reputation for myself or to gain public acclaim or to get what I want. It is no wonder you have withheld your authority from me at times.

God, give me your power to love and to live meekly and humbly, as you will.

Your attitude should be the same as that of Christ Jesus: Who, being in very nature God, did not consider equality with God something to be grasped, but made himself nothing, taking the very nature of a servant, being made in human likeness. And being found in appearance as a man, he humbled himself and became obedient to death—even death on a cross! (Philippians 2:5-8).

Sitting down, Jesus called the Twelve and said, "If anyone wants to be first, he must be the very last, and the servant of all" (Mark 9:35).

Jesus Never Used His Power for Himself

God, why did you honor Jesus as a man in His believing faith? There are no recorded times when Jesus used your power in the realm of the supernatural unless it was directed to meet the need of another person. He never used the power on Himself. Even in the midst of temptation when He could have used your power to meet a logical need such as turning rocks into bread because He was hungry, He refused. Divine working faith in the realm of your power is only to be used in behalf of another, never for self.

"Do you refuse to speak to me?" Pilate said. "Don't you realize I have power either to free you or to crucify you?" Jesus answered, "You would have no power over me if it were not given to you from above. Therefore the one who handed me over to you is guilty of a greater sin" (John 19:10,11).

Power belongs to God (Psalm 62:11, RSV).

"But that you may know that the Son of Man has authority on earth to forgive sins. . . ." He said to the paralytic, "I tell you, get up, take your mat and go home." He got up, took his mat and walked out in full view of them all. This amazed everyone and they praised God, saying, "We have never seen anything like this!" (Mark 2:10-12).

PRAISE

A Love Conversation

It is evening.

As I look into the sky I see that the heavens declare your glory, God. The nights lately have been breathtaking. I have thought about there being over 10,000 billion galaxies with trillions of stars and your Word says you call *each one* by name.

Truly the psalmist was right when he wrote, "What is man that you are mindful of him?"

Father, I love you. I thank you tonight for your lovingkindness that you bring each morning and your faithfulness in the evening.

The heavens declare the glory of God; the skies proclaim the work of his hands (Psalm 19:1).
He determines the number of the stars and calls them each by name (Psalm 147:4).
It is good to praise the Lord and make music to your name, O Most High, to proclaim your love in the morning and your faithfulness at night (Psalm 92:1,2).

PRAYER

True Growth

I think one of the reasons I have not been more effective in helping men grow spiritually is my lack of prayer for those men.

The prayer of a righteous man is powerful and effective (James 5:16).

PREDESTINED

What a Privilege!

What a privilege! You chose Adam to be the first man.
What a privilege! You chose Moses to give your law.
What a privilege! You chose David to be your king.
What a privilege! You chose Elijah to perform your miracles.

Now you have chosen me to be like your Son, to be your son in thought, word and deed. WHAT A PRIVILEGE!

In love he predestined us to be adopted as his sons through Jesus Christ (Ephesians 1:4,5).
When Christ, who is your life, appears, then you also will appear with him in glory (Colossians 3:4).

PRIDE

Presumption in the Midst of Struggles

I have no nervousness when I play Ron in racket ball, but am very nervous when I play Gary. I am totally confident I can beat Ron so I don't even need to make it a matter of praying to you about it. However, I'm afraid Gary will beat me and embarrass me, so I pray to you to give me a good showing when I play him. I notice that all the Christian qualities come out in me when I am the winner, but I have a feeling of discomfort when I lose.

The example of Ron and Gary tells me I must be careful about choosing self-dependence rather than your dependence. You will ultimately destroy my presumption in any situation where I think I am sufficient without you.

I must be very careful of my pride which says, "I will do this or that," instead of having a heart attitude which says, "If the Lord wills . . ."

Pride goes before destruction, a haughty spirit before a fall (Proverbs 16:18).
A man's pride brings him low, but a man of lowly spirit gains honor (Proverbs 29:23).

My Real Problem

Pride permeates our society. Lord, when I am in the midst of struggling with my pride, it seems that the root problem within me is my inability to accept life as a gift. My pride focuses on what I have done instead of what I have received. Paul said, "What do you have that you did not receive; and if you received it, why do you boast as though it is something you attained yourself?"

Father, you say that "a man can receive nothing unless it is given to him from above." It seems that our attitudes would reflect a more grateful spirit if we were to spend more time focusing on what we have rather than on what we don't have. Lord, help me see that "the earth is the Lord's . . . and all that is in it."

And you give whatever you wish to whomever you choose.

A man can receive only what is given him from heaven (John 3:27).
Every good and perfect gift is from above, coming down from the Father of the heavenly lights, who does not change like shifting shadows (James 1:17).

PROBLEMS

Growth Through Problem-Solving

A man gains the important and necessary characteristics of self-worth and personal esteem by having a productive life. He feels empty if he lacks responsible accomplishments.

Much of the insight a person gains is the result of working out the solutions to his own problems. Working through these problems, Lord, gives me maturity, self-worth and self-esteem. I can be enthused about working through problems, for I know that the result will be exciting insights from the Scriptures.

Praise be to the God and Father of our Lord Jesus Christ, the Father of compassion and the God of all comfort, who comforts us in all our troubles, so that we can comfort those in any trouble with the comfort we ourselves have received from God (2 Corinthians 1:3,4).

. . . to be made new in the attitude of your minds; and to put on the new self, created to be like God in true righteousness and holiness (Ephesians 4:23,24).

A sluggard does not plow in season; so at harvest time he looks but finds nothing (Proverbs 20:4).

PROCRASTINATION

Me: The Procrastinator

If you were to come back today, Lord, how much would you discover that I should have done but have procrastinated?

My heart stands condemned today as I think of so many little things you have prompted me to do that I have not done. Help me to live with the motivation that you will come this evening. Help me to put into practice the "Today" principle in being obedient in those areas you wish to change in me.

So, as the Holy Spirit says: "Today, if you hear his voice . . ."
(Hebrews 3:7).
But encourage one another daily, as long as it is called Today, so that none of you may be hardened by sin's deceitfulness (Hebrews 3:13).
But the man who looks intently into the perfect law that gives freedom, and continues to do this, not forgetting what he has heard, but doing it—he will be blessed in what he does (James 1:25).
Anyone, then, who knows the good he ought to do and doesn't do it, sins (James 4:17).

REBELLION

When My Rebellion Makes Me Hurt

I am fearful of writing today because of where I am emotionally as a person, your son and a husband. My mind seems to be totally focused on *my* point of view which is accompanied by a hard-headedness which says, "I am right." When I always am saying I am right, my spirit is ignoring all the biblical principles that tell me to see things from your point of view and to respond accordingly.

Heavenly Father, I sense a rebellious heart toward you and your way in this matter. I am focusing on the scene here and now and not on what you may desire to accomplish 10 to 20 years from now in my life. The truth of my rebellion in this situation comes from knowing your desires, but choosing to say no to them.

I must think of your love for me. You knew me before and loved me. You know me now and love me. You know me best and love me most. How can I doubt that your love now is anything but good and best for me, when I need only look back upon the years of your faithfulness to me? Am I playing the fool by doubting? All your ways toward me have been motivated by your faithfulness and lovingkindness toward me. Oh, my soul, He and His ways alone can be trusted!

Weeping may remain for a night, but rejoicing comes in the morning (Psalm 30:5).
I am still confident of this: I will see the goodness of the Lord in the land of the living (Psalm 27:13).

RELATIONSHIP

True Freedom in Interpersonal Relationships

Father, I sense no fear in relationships when the following attitudes exist:

1. When I desire nothing from the person.

2. When I expect no praise or approval from the person; in reality, this means I'm not trying to get him to like me or to be impressed with me.

3. When my focus is to *give*, not get, no matter what the consequence.

These attitudes give me the motive of seeking the other person's best and not my personal glory.

I pray that I will have this freedom in all relationships with others, so that I can express your love more clearly.

So we say with confidence, "The Lord is my helper; I will not be afraid. What can man do to me? (Hebrews 13:6).
It is surely obvious that something must be seriously wrong in your church for you to be having lawsuits at all. Why not let yourself be wronged or cheated? For when you go to law against your brother you yourself do him wrong, for you cheat him of Christian love and forgiveness. Have you forgotten that the kingdom of God will never belong to the wicked? Don't be under any illusion—neither the impure, the idolator or the adulterer; neither the effeminate, the pervert or the thief; neither the swindler, the drunkard, the foul-mouthed or the rapacious shall have any share in the kingdom of God
(1 Corinthians 6:7-10 Phillips).

Past the Halfway Point

I'm several days past 35—this may be the halfway point of my life as measured by the biblical "threescore and ten." What a shame to think of all the selfish moments in those 35 years which will have no lasting worth from the viewpoint of eternal values!

One of the keys to my life in the next 35 years will be my relationship with my wife. I need much growth in my relationship with her. I must meditate on what you desire for our own good. I see your will in your love for us and I desire to function within that will. However, I also see a grip on my will which often pulls me back when I want to move forward.

I'm in the midst of a struggle. Father, I seek a changed attitude that will bring you joy and that will be an encouragement to my wife.

Husbands, in the same way be considerate as you live with your wives, and treat them with respect as the weaker partner and as heirs with you of the gracious gift of life, so that nothing will hinder your prayers (1 Peter 3:7).

RESPONSIBILITY

Experiencing Failure at Home

Father, lately I have had a great sense of personal failure and defeat in my home life. Both of us have many needs to be fulfilled. We want you at the center of our relationship. Paul says to wake up to reality and live responsibly. I must do this with my family during times of conflict.

Live life, then, with a due sense of responsibility, not as men who do not know the meaning and purpose of life but as those who do (Ephesians 5:15, Phillips).

SACRIFICE

God Desires a Living Sacrifice

Your desire that I be a *living sacrifice* is to prove to the world that your will, which will be worked out in me, is GOOD, ACCEPTABLE and PERFECT.

A sacrifice-motivation is not one which asks, "What will I gain or lose personally?" Rather, its focus is to be what *you* will gain or lose by doing or not doing something.

Without faith it will be impossible for me to offer myself wholly to you. None of the joy of faith is seen in the seeing world, but that doesn't matter to me; for in the reality of the unseen world I will experience your good, acceptable and perfect will if I choose to be a living sacrifice. Praise you, God, that the unseen is the truth of the universe, while the seen and all it offers is many times a lie.

Therefore, I urge you, brothers, in view of God's mercy, to offer your bodies as living sacrifices, holy and pleasing to God—which is your spiritual worship (Romans 12:1).
And without faith it is impossible to please God, because anyone who comes to him must believe that he exists and that he rewards those who earnestly seek him (Hebrews 11:6).

SELF-PITY

When My Eyes Turn Inward

I have an intense feeling of self-pity today. I am involved with people, but have an acute sense of loneliness even in the midst of a crowd. My problem seems to be because my thoughts are focused inwardly rather than outwardly, for I am comparing myself with those more talented than I am.

Why are you downcast, O my soul? Why so disturbed within me? Put your hope in God, for I will yet praise him, my Savior and my God (Psalm 43:5).

How long, O Lord? Will you forget me forever? How long will you hide your face from me? How long must I wrestle with my thoughts and every day have sorrow in my heart? How long will my enemy triumph over me? (Psalm 13:1,2).

We do not dare to classify or compare ourselves with some who commend themselves. When they measure themselves by themselves and compare themselves with themselves, they are not wise (2 Corinthians 10:12).

SERVANTHOOD
My True Self

The true meaning of a man's life can be revealed by
that which he thinks about when alone. Also, what I am
as a man is revealed by how I act when with people who
can be of no benefit to me. What am I like when I am
with people from whom I want nothing?

*Now that I, your Lord and Teacher, have washed your feet,
you also should wash one another's feet. I have set you an
example that you should do as I have done for you (John
13:14,15).*
*. . . just as the Son of Man did not come to be served, but to
serve . . . (Matthew 20:28).*
*He will reply, "I tell you the truth, whatever you did not do for
one of the least of these, you did not do for me" (Matthew
25:45).*
*Let us have no imitation Christian love. . . . Let us have real
warm affection for one another as between brothers, and a
willingness to let the other man have the credit (Romans
12:9,10, Phillips).*

The Ultimate in Servanthood

Judas was a thief. Jesus knew it, but He still served him and washed his feet.

Please, Father, encourage me in such a way that I will do good to the man who I feel has wronged me. Thank you for the practical situation in which I can bless him who is cursing me. May I strive in private circles only to lift him up and to do good to him anonymously.

Do not repay evil with evil or insult with insult, but with blessing, because to this you were called so that you may inherit a blessing (1 Peter 3:9).

The greatest among you will be your servant. For whoever exalts himself will be humbled, and whoever humbles himself will be exalted (Matthew 23:11,12).

When they hurled their insults at him, he did not retaliate; when he suffered, he made no threats (1 Peter 2:23).

SPIRITUAL GIFTS

Understanding Others' Ways of Doing Things

I need to understand the purpose of a thing before I can discern its true meaning. I must ask myself the question of why I do this or that.

I need to clearly realize that people with different gifts have different answers to the question of "Why?" Within the Body of Christ, many of us tend to evaluate others according to our strengths and judge others according to our weaknesses. If my spiritual gift is evangelism, then I must not be too hasty in evaluating others based upon how or even whether or not they actively share Christ. Their answer to why, which determines their purpose in life, may come from another gift, such as the gift of mercy or helps or teaching or something else. It is good to know that their motivation for joy, which comes from exercising one's spiritual gift, will be different from mine; yet it will be fully within the God-given purpose for their life.

Jesus answered, "You are right in saying I am a king. In fact, for this reason I was born, and for this I came into the world, to testify to the truth (John 18:37).
There are different kinds of gifts, but the same Spirit. There are different kinds of service, but the same Lord. There are different kinds of working, but the same God works all of them in all men (I Corinthians 12:4-6).

STANDARDS

His Standards Versus the World's Standards

Jesus, in John 14 you say that Satan, the ruler of *this* world, is coming and he has no hold on you as he does on people of the world. I see the street people hustling for a dollar. They feel comfortable doing it because everyone else is doing it. Your Word says you will cause many to stumble because you will establish such a high standard that they must attack you in order to soothe their convicted conscience at the type of life they lead.

Oh, if by unmerited grace I could present a quality of life that would draw or split groups for your name's sake!

I will not speak with you much longer, for the prince of this world is coming. He has no hold on me, but the world must learn that I love the Father and that I do exactly what my Father has commanded me (John 14:30,31).

This child is destined to make many fall and many rise in Israel and to set up a standard which many will attack—for he will expose the secret thoughts of many hearts (Luke 2:34, Phillips).

SUBMISSION

The Meaning of True Submission

Lord, Isaac's attitudes should be evaluated during the time Abraham offered him as a sacrifice. What submission to lie on that stack of wood, when he could have physically overpowered his father! But he willingly submitted, clearly being able to see his father raise the knife to kill him.

What a life-changing experience for a son to submit to his father's faith in the God he had taught him about!

What can I learn from this? Not only to have the heart of Isaac, as you my heavenly Father lead me, but also to have a life that will cause my daughter to trust my God as I obey you, as Isaac trusted his father's God.

Though he slay me, yet will I hope in him (Job 13:15).

When I Secretly Expect My Way

Lord, I say I will give my all to you, but in return I secretly expect you to use me in a special way. When you don't fulfill my expectations based upon my sacrificial offer of my life to you, I often become bitter and resentful. I must learn to lay my all before you and expect *nothing* but only to be available to you for whatever you choose to do with my life.

Wait for the Lord; be strong and take heart and wait for the Lord (Psalm 27:14).

TEMPTATION

Battlefields

Sex, sensuality and immorality are everywhere. There truly is pleasure in sin for a season. Man's only hope is to see his decisions as they would appear 100 years from now. Are a few moments of pleasure worth compromising God's best for eternity? How we try to subdue each other and impress each other for the purpose of conquering the other for selfish gain!

No wonder you chose Moses. Few men in history have chosen to walk away from being the most powerful and richest on earth. But Moses did. He "looked steadily at the ultimate, not the immediate, reward."

Oh, that my frame of reference in business and life would be not that which is seen, but that which is unseen. Help me realize that life is a vapor, that I am merely a passer-through, a sojourner, a citizen of another world—and to remember that what I think and say are examined and exposed in your presence.

These attitudes seem hard now, but if I could talk with Moses or Peter or Paul, they would cry out to the worth of them.

I must learn to become reckless in my faith!

Dear friends, I urge you, as aliens and strangers in the world, to abstain from sinful desires, which war against your soul (1 Peter 2:11).
So we fix our eyes not on what is seen, but on what is unseen. For what is seen is temporary, but what is unseen is eternal (2 Corinthians 4:18).
He considered the "reproach of Christ" more precious than all the wealth of Egypt, for he looked steadily at the ultimate, not the immediate, reward (Hebrews 11:26, Phillips).

Being on Guard for Satan's Traps

Lord, it seems that every basic need you have given man becomes the source of every major temptation from Satan:

My need for sex—Satan tries to get me to exercise this need outside of your boundaries of marriage.

My need for food—Satan tries to get me to make my belly my god through gluttony.

My need for self-esteem and self-worth—Satan tries to get me to receive the honor and glory of man by conforming to man's ways.

For, as I have often told you before and now say again even with tears, many live as enemies of the cross of Christ. Their destiny is destruction, their god is their stomach, and their glory is in their shame (Philippians 3:18,19).

Be self-controlled and alert. Your enemy the devil prowls around like a roaring lion looking for someone to devour. Resist him (1 Peter 5:8,9).

The Unknown Impact of Culture

I'm back on the road today. What a sense of loneliness I have out here in these different cities when I'm by myself. Satan starts the attack as soon as I get to the literature area of the airport: sex and sensuality are everywhere. I sense a little of what the book of 2 Peter is saying when it speaks of Lot's righteous soul being in torment when he lived in Sodom and Gomorrah. Even though he didn't succumb to it, it affected him subconsciously when he later offered his daughters to be raped in order to protect his honored guests. Father, when I'm alone my hope is in the faithfulness of your Holy Spirit's overruling the lust of my flesh.

Do not love the world or anything in the world. If anyone loves the world, the love of the Father is not in him. For everything in the world—the cravings of sinful man, the lust of his eyes and the boasting of what he has and does—comes not from the Father but from the world (1 John 2:15,16).
And if he rescued Lot, a righteous man, who was distressed by the filthy lives of lawless men (for that righteous man, living among them day after day, was tormented in his righteous soul by the lawless deeds he saw and heard) . . . then the Lord knows how to rescue godly men from trials (2 Peter 2:7-9).

The Signal to Turn to God

Temptation should only be a signal, God, from you—a signal allowing the forces of evil to attack us, *so that we then may consciously turn our attention back to you.*

When I am tempted, I immediately need to go to you and bring every thought to your attention. This will be letting Satan know that when he assaults me, he will be sending me directly to the glory of the cross which brought his ultimate defeat.

For though we live in the world, we do not wage war as the world does. The weapons we fight with are not the weapons of the world. On the contrary, they have divine power to demolish strongholds. We demolish arguments and every pretension that sets itself up against the knowledge of God, and we take captive every thought to make it obedient to Christ (2 Corinthians 10:3-5).

What Are the Roots?

Temptation is seated in the assumption that you are withholding your best from me. I become envious and curious as I look at the prosperity of the wicked, for they seem to have everything people want. And while the wicked prosper, I, a believer of your truth, seem to have nothing but trouble. However, there is a big difference, for your Word shows that "even in laughter the heart may ache, and joy may end in grief" (Proverbs 14:13).

Instead of believing the unseen of the scriptural truths as I should be doing, I often tend to believe what I see. I become curious about all the fun and laughter of the wicked. You tell me not to be envious of the wicked, for the end of their path is death. Why do I sometimes conclude that your way is wrong and that you are really withholding the best of life from me, when, actually, all my joy in life has only come through your faithful lovingkindness.

All the ways of the Lord are loving and faithful for those who keep the demands of his covenant (Psalm 25:10).
But as for me, my feet had almost slipped; I had nearly lost my foothold. For I envied the arrogant when I saw the prosperity of the wicked" (Psalm 73:2,3).
Yet because the wicked do not fear God, it will not go well with them (Ecclesiastes 8:13).

When Grace Is Truly Sufficient

I am in Boston today. What loneliness and anger in the faces of people! I'm really having to struggle with sin and sensuality. I received a note from a girl on the plane. She wrote her phone number and wanted me to call her. What a battle not to! I too am lonely; but, praise you, Lord, for your faithful spiritual presence which rises up each time I'm tempted. You give your grace to meet the situation in victory for your name's sake.

No temptation has seized you except what is common to man. And God is faithful; he will not let you be tempted beyond what you can bear. But when you are tempted, he will also provide a way out so that you can stand up under it (1 Corinthians 10:13).
For the lips of an adulteress drip honey, and her speech is smoother than oil; but in the end she is bitter as gall, sharp as a double-edged sword. Her feet go down to death; her steps lead straight to the grave (Proverbs 5:3-5).

TROUBLE

Trouble—Often God's Best

Paul was compelled by the Holy Spirit to go to Rome, and what awaited him there was imprisonment and persecution. He was led into "trouble." Many times when we feel we have the Spirit's leadership in a matter we get excited but begin to doubt when trouble develops. Father, if I move with your conviction, I must trust you for whatever you give me when I arrive.

Now I want you to know, brothers, that what has happened to me has really served to advance the gospel. As a result, it has become clear throughout the whole palace guard and to everyone else that I am in chains for Christ. Because of my chains, most of the brothers in the Lord have been encouraged to speak the word of God more courageously and fearlessly (Philippians 1:12-14).

Dear friends, do not be surprised at the painful trial you are suffering, as though something strange were happening to you. But rejoice that you participate in the sufferings of Christ, so that you may be overjoyed when his glory is revealed (1 Peter 4:12,13).

TRUST

Why I Can't Trust People Who Say They Love Me

I can't trust or believe people who say they love me if I know that my life has been a pretense to them. I conclude that they don't really know me; they only know who I have pretended to be.

No wonder I say that I can't trust them when they say they love me. The problem is not in their acceptance of me; the problem is accepting myself enough to expose the real me.

But he said to me, "My grace is sufficient for you, for my power is made perfect in weakness." Therefore I will boast all the more gladly about my weaknesses, so that Christ's power may rest on me (2 Corinthians 12:9).

Don't cherish exaggerated ideas of yourself or your importance, but try to have a sane estimate of your capabilities by the light of faith that God has given to you all (Romans 12:3, Phillips).

When I Don't Think I Need Him

Humanly speaking, when we think we have a good deal, there is a tendency to think inwardly that we don't need you in the matter. Father, I reject these inward conclusions which come from my flesh and ask you to work in the company's behalf to allow us to sell this property in the next month. My trust is in you and not in the deal or myself.

Trust in the Lord with all your heart and lean not on your own understanding; in all your ways acknowledge him, and he will make your paths straight (Proverbs 3:5,6).

God Keeps the Books

I have a debt of sin and need to pay the debt with a credit of righteousness. I cannot do this myself, but you made a bookkeeping entry that credited to my account Christ's righteousness. You were legally able to do that because the debt was paid by Christ. If I simply reorganize my debt obligation for my sin, acknowledging that Christ said He would pay it and trusting that He did, then you make that bookkeeping entry in your heavenly records.

Thanks for so great a salvation that cost you so much to offer a free gift to me.

However, to the man who does not work but trusts God who justifies the wicked, his faith is credited as righteousness (Romans 4:5).
God made him who had no sin to be sin for us, so that in him we might become the righteousness of God
(2 Corinthians 5:21).

Making Blind Spots Clear

Father, I can't really deal with my problems until you point to the specifics and give me a conscious handle to work with. I can't sense the problem until clear insight is given to the area of doubt. Until then, I must trust you with it and rest in the fact that you *will* deal with it in your own way and time.

I must relax in the confidence that I am where you want me to be now; that you alone are committed to reveal those areas in my life which need to be changed, but changed in your time.

How I need to be confident of being in your will and to be excited that I am right now where you want me to be. And, if I am not, you are responsible to get me there with a willing heart. How this frees me from the tension of always struggling with the thought, "Am I in your will; am I where you want me to be?"

But by the grace of God I am what I am, and his grace to me was not without effect (2 Corinthians 15:10).
I have much more to say to you, more than you can now bear (John 16:12).
I will instruct you and teach you in the way you should go; I will counsel you and watch over you (Psalm 32:8).

Those Inner Drives

There seems to be a sinful impulsiveness within man that is always driving him to try to satisfy that which can never be satisfied. It can't be fully satisfied, for it is only a pleasure for a moment.

Oh, that I might relax and allow myself to be driven by your Holy Spirit. Do I continue to move forward in the lives of people in order to get or to give? Is it possible to love and not be aggressive with people? Or does love mean that I must always try to take the lead with a person? Is this leadership for spiritual or selfish reasons?

What a privilege it would be to truly trust your Spirit in my life! I see so much disbelief in my life and so much lack of confidence in trusting you, yet you are utterly trustworthy. Father, forgive me of such a great sin as this that claims by my life that you can't or won't seek my best. How that must grieve you! I am deeply sorrowful I have grieved you. Please forgive me.

And I will ask the Father, and he will give you another Counselor to be with you forever—the Spirit of truth. The world cannot accept him, because it neither sees him nor knows him. But you know him, for he lives with you and will be in you (John 14:16,17).
And I—in righteousness I will see your face; when I awake, I will be satisfied with seeing your likeness (Psalm 17:15).
All man's efforts are for his mouth, yet his appetite is never satisfied (Ecclesiastes 6:7).

TRUTH

Every Man Is to Be a Standard

Jesus, you said you came into the world to witness to the truth. Luke 2 says of you, "His destiny is to cause many people to rise and many to fall because He will set up a standard which many will attack, for He will expose the motives of men's hearts."

Truth can be the only criterion for my business deals. I must have such a commitment to truth that my word can be trusted at all costs, even if I lose a great deal financially. My return on this commitment will far outreach any momentary financial success or loss.

Yet because I tell the truth, you can not believe me! Can any of you prove me guilty of sin? If I am telling the truth, why don't you believe me? (John 8:45,46).
Lord, who may dwell in your sanctuary? Who may live on your holy hill? He whose walk is blameless and who does what is righteous, who speaks the truth from his heart . . . who keeps his oath even when it hurts (Psalm 15:1,2,4).

WEAKNESSES
When I Play the Role of the Fool

Oh, my soul, why don't you speak in accordance with what you believe? My mind says, "True"; my heart yells, "Yes"; but my mouth holds its peace because my will cannot stand to be rejected—or because I cannot stand to be thought of as anything other than a "neat guy." What a fool I am, Lord, to want to be praised by the world for the momentary pleasure of self! I then lose your applause, which lasts for eternity!

Stand firm in one spirit, contending as one man for the faith of the gospel without being frightened in any way by those who oppose you. This is a sign to them that they will be destroyed, but that you will be saved—and that by God (Philippians 1:27,28).
For it seems to me that God has put us apostles on display at the end of the procession, like men condemned to die in the arena. We have been made a spectacle to the whole universe, to angels as well as to men. We are fools for Christ, but you are so wise in Christ! We are weak, but you are strong! You are honored, we are dishonored! . . . When we are slandered, we answer kindly. Up to this moment we have become the scum of the earth, the refuse of the world (1 Corinthians 4:9,10,13).

Openness, the Key to Honesty

A man must understand his weaknesses and not try to hide them from himself and from you. Confidence must come in the quiet understanding of who I am (both good and bad, strong and weak), so I will be honest in your presence.

Let us not be ambitious for our own reputations, for that only means making one another jealous (Galatians 5:26, Phillips). Therefore I will boast all the more gladly about my weaknesses, so that Christ's power may rest on me. That is why, for Christ's sake, I delight in weaknesses, in insults, in hardships, in persecutions, in difficulties. For when I am weak, then I am strong (2 Corinthians 12:9,10).

But the meek will inherit the land and enjoy great peace (Psalm 37:11).

WITNESSING

Being Useful to You in Spite of Myself

I met Warren on the plane trip to New York—a trip I didn't want to take. He digs clams on Long Island and all he wanted to know as we talked about the gospel was, "How do I receive Him?" He told me several times to keep explaining and to show him how to receive Jesus Christ. I pray, Father, as the angels are now rejoicing over his salvation, that you will lead someone to him to help him grow in grace and truth, so that Warren will reproduce what has happened to him in the lives of others.

Father, what an encouragement you give me when all I was doing was complaining about this trip I had to take. Teach me to trust you as you tell me that my steps are to be ordered by you. What a privilege to be used by the Spirit when I was actually angry at you.

We are therefore Christ's ambassadors, as though God were making his appeal through us. We implore you on Christ's behalf: Be reconciled to God (2 Corinthians 5:20).
Though I am free and belong to no man, I make myself a slave to everyone, to win as many as possible. To the weak I became weak, to win the weak. I have become all things to all men so that by all possible means I might save some
(1 Corinthians 9:19,22).

The Right Type of Impatience

How can I be patient with people who I know are lost and who need to have their lives changed by an encounter with Christ? Lord, cause me to walk in such a way that my life would be as salt that causes people to thirst for the life that Jesus Christ alone can bring to a man.

You are the salt of the earth. But if the salt loses its saltiness, how can it be made salty again? It is no longer good for anything, except to be thrown out and trampled by men (Matthew 5:13).
In the same way, let your light shine before men, that they may see your good deeds and praise your Father in heaven (Matthew 5:16).
But thanks be to God, who always leads us in triumphal procession in Christ and through us spreads everywhere the fragrance of the knowledge of him. For we are to God the aroma of Christ among those who are being saved and those who are perishing (2 Corinthians 2:14,15).

Nothing Happens Without You

On the airplane today I talked to a man who calls himself a Jewish atheist. He is closed to everything about you, Lord Jesus. No matter what techniques we use in sharing the gospel, it is evident that no true spiritual activity takes place unless you act. There have been times, Father, when I have perhaps given an ineffective explanation, yet men were brought to you *because of your activity in the midst of the situation.*

Give me a heavenly boldness to speak out for Christ, even if all I can do is simply tell of His love that I have personally experienced.

Though I am free and belong to no man, I make myself a slave to everyone, to win as many as possible (1 Corinthians 9:19). The wind blows wherever it pleases. You hear its sound, but you cannot tell where it comes from or where it is going. So it is with everyone born of the Spirit (John 3:8).

Being Unaware of God's Use of Us

Much of Paul's writings came from his personal experience. By making those writings your holy Word, you are saying that these letters to New Testament Christians involve your will for *all men*—even today.

Paul seemingly had no idea that his letters would be thought of as your Word in the same sense as the Old Testament. Accordingly, what we say and how we are involved with people will have impacts unknown to us if our lives are lived in your light.

But if we walk in the light, as he is in the light, we have fellowship with one another (1 John 1:7).
Whoever of you loves life and desires to see many good days, keep your tongue from evil and your lips from speaking lies. Turn from evil and do good; seek peace and pursue it (Psalm 34:12-14).

God's Creativeness in Conversation

While having dinner later tonight with a client, I ask that you open a natural sequence of conversation so we may discuss you, Lord, in a relaxed way. Make me sensitive to know when and when not to speak.

Those who had been scattered preached the word wherever they went (Acts 8:4).
But in your hearts set apart Christ as Lord. Always be prepared to give an answer to everyone who asks you to give the reason for the hope that you have (1 Peter 3:15).

A Divine Appointment

I met a man from Poland today on the train to Zurich. What a divine appointment! He was really open to the claims of Christ even though he had never heard about God as he grew up. Thank you, Father, for the privilege to share Christ with this man. I never cease to be amazed at how you develop these divine appointments to meet the needs of those you intend to bring to yourself. Give him no rest until he finds his rest in you.

How, then, can they call on the one they have not believed in? And how can they believe in the one of whom they have not heard? And how can they hear without someone preaching to them? And how can they preach unless they are sent? As it is written, "How beautiful are the feet of those who bring good news!" (Romans 10:14,15).
Restore to me the joy of your salvation and grant me a willing spirit, to sustain me. Then I will teach transgressors your ways, and sinners will turn back to you (Psalm 51:12,13).

Reaping the Harvest

Gary is very open to spiritual issues. Father, I trust that our paths may cross again so I may clearly explain how he can know you. I continue to pray that I can share with his sister, for she is open also.

Thank you for Gary's openness and the privilege of simply reaping a harvest that time and emptiness had prepared. I hope his family will be sensitive to the change that is already there.

"Come, follow me," Jesus said, "and I will make you fishers of men" (Matthew 4:19).
I am not ashamed of the gospel, because it is the power of God for the salvation of everyone who believes (Romans 1:16).

The Meaning of True Acceptance

As I am exposed to the crowd in New York this week, I ask you to make my life refreshing to them in a way that will allow me to speak the truth in love. Let me present your way and your love to them. Let them know I love them and accept them whether they trust you or not.

Most of all, let me not be deceived by Satan to think I must do what they do so they will listen to what I say. Your light cannot mix with darkness, so give me the courage to be free and bold and to have the ability to stand alone for your name's sake.

I love you, Father. The hope of victory and honor unto you is in you.

Flee the evil desires of youth, and pursue righteousness, faith, love and peace, along with those who call on the Lord out of a pure heart. Don't have anything to do with foolish and stupid arguments, because you know they produce quarrels. And the Lord's servant must not quarrel; instead, he must be kind to everyone, able to teach, not resentful. Those who oppose him he must gently instruct, in the hope that God will grant them repentance leading them to a knowledge of the truth, and that they will come to their senses and escape from the trap of the devil, who has taken them captive to do his will (2 Timothy 2:22-26).

Since, then, we know what it is to fear the Lord, we try to persuade men. What we are is plain to God, and I hope it is also plain to your conscience. So from now on we regard no one from a worldly point of view (2 Corinthians 5:11, 16).

When We Are Available to Share Christ

J.F. trusted Christ today in the hotel restaurant. What a lesson in trusting you for the right timing for the salvation of a friend! You are so creative in developing just the proper circumstances. You create the right type of pressures to cause people to be willing to listen to answers to questions they have been afraid to ask most of their lives.

It helped when my companion, Ron, told of his decision for you. It gives great strength to a witnessing encounter when another publicly confesses you.

Thank you that J.F. was honest in admitting that even though he was "religious" he had never trusted you alone as Saviour.

What a joy to share in the work of such a lasting achievement as being involved with those you bring to yourself.

We proclaim him, admonishing and teaching everyone with all wisdom, so that we may present everyone perfect in Christ. To this end I labor, struggling with all his energy, which so powerfully works in me (Colossians 1:28,29).
Whoever acknowledges me before men, I will also acknowledge him before my Father in heaven (Matthew 10:32).

WORRY

Surfacing True Feelings

I talked with a bullish economist at the bank today about whether or not to hold our property. But my spirit is not free on the issue. Why? Am I reputation-conscious? Do I want out of the pressure? Am I afraid of what my investors think of me if they should lose money? Am I concerned about my reputation if I should give wrong investment counsel?

Search me, Lord, and try my motives.

"Martha, Martha," the Lord answered, *"you are worried and upset about many things"* (Luke 10:41).
Who of you by worrying can add a single hour to his life? (Matthew 6:27).

WORSHIP

A Willingness to Stop and Be Still

You say, "Be still, and know that I am God."

You ask me to be alone with you; to be still and think about you. What a privilege to rest and focus on you, Lord Jesus, and your ways! What freedom a person may have if his goal is only to live for you. Most of the little games we get involved in will disappear. The freedom to live in the light of the truth and not a life of lies is so exhilarating compared to the phoniness we extend when we want approval, recognition, attention, honor and glory.

Lord, grip your people in our society in such a way so as to keep us in a holy fear of the danger of missing what true reality is. Cause us to be willing to stop and be still so we have time to address the honest questions we so often run away from. We escape answering them because we are so busy doing the "urgent" things in life that we do not have time to dwell on the "important" questions for which there are no easy answers.

Sometimes we feel that if we don't face the deeper questions—about death, you and eternity—that they will go away. Help us to bring them into the light of life so we can deal with them openly.

Then you will know the truth, and the truth will set you free (John 8:32).
Yet I am writing you a new command; its truth is seen in him and you, because the darkness is passing and the true light is already shining (1 John 2:8).
Be still, and know that I am God (Psalm 46:10).

The Ruthless Maze of Activity

I listened to a tape just now on how to seek you. I really needed to hear this. My life has been a maze of activity that briefly seems to touch only a few people in a very shallow way. I need to be *still* and silent before you, Father. Everything has come before you recently, and even though it was activity for the Kingdom, I have missed the mark in regard to worshiping and fellowshiping with you.

Please forgive me (and I know you have). Thank you for intervening before I became too stretched out and starved. When I say, "I thirst, Lord Jesus," your command is "Come to me." May my response be, "I come."

Be still, and know that I am God (Psalm 46:10).
Come to me, all you who are weary and burdened, and I will give you rest. Take my yoke upon you and learn from me, for I am gentle and humble in heart, and you will find rest for your souls (Matthew 11:28,29).

Index

ACKNOWLEDGEMENT

The Scripture says that he who walks with wise men becomes wise. A deep sense of gratitude is felt by me for the godly men God has brought me in contact with over the last 10 years, but especially the ones He's allowed me to be partners with in various business opportunities. Much thanks to Richard Ford, Tom Crocker, and my present partner Pat Booth for their love, encouragement, and patience during our business enterprises with a man who has a history of being a slow learner. Thanks to Chuck Unger who helped tremendously on editing the diaries and to Don Meredith, Jody Dillow and many other faithful friends who encouraged me to make these thoughts available in book form.